the Way Home

"A truly refreshing perspective from a man who desires to be real about the struggles we all too often try to conceal. Wayne has lit the torch with a flame of passion that is sure to ignite anyone who desires a deeper relationship with our Lord and Savior Jesus Christ."

—**Kent Bottenfield**, relief pitcher for the St. Louis Cardinals

"Wayne Watson has the gift of godly words that express what we so often feel or need in our relationship with God. *The Way Home* touches us where we need it—in our hearts. It reminds us over and again of our desperate need of Christ and his grace."

—**Jim Cymbala**, Pastor, The Brooklyn Tabernacle

"This book combines Wayne's musical writing abilities and his knowledge of the Word and can help transform a mediocre Christian into a truly godly one."

—**Steve Jones**, PGA Tour golf professional

"For years we have enjoyed his songs and music. Now Wayne takes us deeper into the life issues and biblical origins of his lyrics. There are lessons here for everyone wanting to walk more closely with God. These life applications will surely benefit all who read them."

—**Dr. Boyd D. Lyles Jr.**, Cooper Clinic

"Wayne Watson's devotional book, *The Way Home,* caused me to pause, ponder and reflect on my life and spiritual direction. It's packed with the same unique insights that I find deeply stirring in Wayne's music. It's great! Grab it, and take it all the way home!

—**Ken Ruettgers**, 12-year veteran of Green Bay Packers and author of *Homefield Advantage*

"Wayne Watson's life and words have always been an encouragement to me. I know that I will not grow in the Lord unless I am challenged to do so. *The Way Home* does just that. This book is a reflection of Wayne's personal desire to be more like Jesus and a call for all of us to be that as well."

—**Michael Omartian**, multi-Grammy award winning record producer

"Wayne Watson has a way of talking to us in a down-to-earth, heartfelt way in his music and now in his devotional book. *The Way Home* hits us right where we live and challenges us to think more about our lives in Jesus."

—**Tim Burke**, former Major League All-Star pitcher and author of *Major League Dad*

INSPIRATIONS OF
A LIFETIME

the Way Home
Wayne Watson

HOWARD
PUBLISHING CO.

THE ARTISTS DEVOTIONAL SERIES

Our purpose at Howard Publishing is to:

- *Increase faith* in the hearts of growing Christians
- *Inspire holiness* in the lives of believers
- *Instill hope* in the hearts of struggling people everywhere

Because He's coming again!

Published by Howard Publishing Co., Inc.,
3117 North 7th Street, West Monroe, Louisiana 71291-2227

98 99 00 01 02 03 04 05 06 07   10 9 8 7 6 5 4 3 2 1

Library of Congress Cataloging-in Publication Data

Watson, Wayne.
    The way home : inspirations of a lifetime / Wayne Watson
        p. cm. — (The artists devotional series)
    ISBN 1-878990-84-5 (alk. paper)
    1. Devotional exercises. I. Title. II. Series.
    BV4832.2.W39 1998
    242—dc21   97-51690

Interior design by LinDee Loveland
Manuscript editing by Philis Boultinghouse

Scripture quotations not otherwise marked are from the New International Version, © 1973, 1978, 1984 by International Bible Society. Used by permission Zondervan Bible Publishers. Scriptures quoted from *The Holy Bible, New Century Version,* copyright © 1987, 1988, 1991 by Word Publishing, Dallas, Texas 75234. Used by permission. Other Scriptures quoted from the New Revised Stardard Version Bible © 1989, Div. of Christian Education of the National Council of the Churches of Christ in the United States of America; Revised Standard Version, Old Testament © 1952, New Testament © 1946 by Div. of Christian Education of the National Council of the Churches of Christ in the United States of America.

∽

To my dad

Contents

بہ

CONTENTS

Contents

Introduction

꒳

I have to confess, my first thought at the proposal of doing a devotional book was (in the words of Snoopy) "Aaar-rrrgghhhh!" In my own meager library, there are more than enough books written by very wise and learned scholars—men and women with great theological backgrounds who have given their perspectives and interpretations of God's Word. So I found myself thinking, "Do we really need another devotional book?"

But it occurred to me that folks who enjoy Christian music might enjoy exploring more deeply the truths touched upon in these three-minute audio wonders. My hope and prayer is that these devotionals will do far more than give you further insight into some songs you might know—that would simply be vanity. But if these writings help you become more familiar with the Savior, see his face more clearly, know his grace beyond the rules of religious tradition, and trust him more in your walk in this busy, modern world, then good will have come from this. I hope that wherever you go, you'll always know "The Way Home."

ONE

Friend
of a
Wounded
Heart

*f*rom the album

WATERCOLOUR PONIES

Friend of a Wounded Heart

Smile, make 'em think you're happy
Lie, and say that things are fine
And hide that empty longing that you feel
Don't ever show it
Just keep your heart concealed

Why are the days so lonely?
Where can the heart go free?
And who will dry the tears that no one's seen?
There must be someone
To share your silent dreams

Caught like a leaf in the wind
Looking for a friend—Where can you turn?
Whisper the words of a prayer

And you'll find him there
Arms open wide—love in his eyes

(Chorus)
Jesus, he meets you where you are
Jesus, he heals your secret scars
All the love you're longing for is
Jesus, the friend of the wounded heart

Joy comes like the morning
Hope deepens as you grow
And peace beyond the reaches of your soul
Comes flowing through you
For love has made you whole

Once like a leaf in the wind
Lookin' for a friend—Where could you turn?
You spoke the words of a prayer
And you found him there
Arms open wide—love in His eyes

(Repeat Chorus)

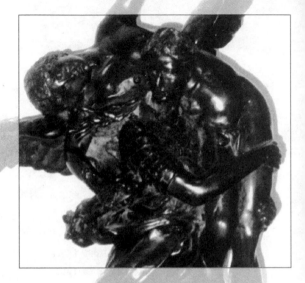

Allow yourself to be carried by the one who offers healing and hope.

Heal me, O Lord, and I will be healed;
save me and I will be saved,
for you are the one I praise.
Jeremiah 17:14

n my living room stands a twenty-inch statue of two figures—one is carrying the other. The standing figure is an angel, strong and muscular, complete with fine wings. Over his shoulder he carries the wounded body of a warrior. In one hand the wounded soldier grips a broken weapon—probably broken in battle.

It's interesting to watch people's reactions when they first see this statue. Without presuming too much, I have to say, I can tell a lot about folks by their reactions.

Some are deeply moved. They are drawn to the statue and seem to feel a close affinity with the wounded man. They know what it is to be wounded, and they know what it is to rely on another.

But others are quietly stunned and just don't seem to get it. While trying to be polite, it's obvious they don't (or can't) appreciate the spiritual implications of the statue. They've either never been badly wounded or don't care to acknowledge their wounds.

All of us know people who don't acknowledge hurts and scars; they live as if ignoring pain will make it go away. In fact, even the most "spiritual" of us have played that role at times. I know I have. You probably have too. The perils of ignoring spiritual and emotional problems can be seen in a physical parallel. It doesn't take an M.D. to know that a deep wound left untreated can start a dangerous chain reaction—sometimes a deadly one! So it is with emotional injuries. If they go untended, they fester and become inflamed, and the infection spreads. A wise person recognizes that the beginning of healing is the acknowledgment of illness.

If you have a wounded heart—and all of us do to some extent or another—know that Jesus has positioned himself as your friend. Through his short lifetime on earth, Christ was not only a friend to sinners but also a healer of broken hearts and broken dreams. Those without hope found encouragement in the presence of the Savior. Those with battered bodies found healing in his touch. Do you remember the woman who simply touched the garment of Jesus and found healing because of her faith? In his presence, you, too, can find healing—even today.

People who see Jesus merely as a historical figure or a religious leader leave his presence untouched and cold. Like those who don't "get" the statue in my living room, they don't understand the reality of what Jesus offers.

See yourself as the wounded warrior carried by the mighty angel. Be willing to acknowledge your pain; allow yourself to be carried by the one who offers healing, hope, and even friendship—Jesus Christ, the Friend of a Wounded Heart.

PERSONAL REFLECTIONS

1. What kind of reaction might you have to the statue in my living room?

2. Do you ever allow yourself to be "carried" by another, or do you always feel that you must be strong and in control?

3. Search your heart. Do you carry any unacknowledged wounds?

4. What wounds in your life has Jesus already healed?

life response

Name any previously unacknowledged wounds that came to mind during this reading. Take them in prayer to the Friend of Wounded Hearts.

TWO

There
Goes
Sundown

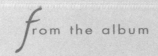

There Goes Sundown

Doomsday—someday
But not today so far
Said this world wouldn't
Be here much longer
But look around, here we are

Only God in his wisdom
Surely not me in mine
Knows the number
Of the days of a man
Every day he shows me a sign

(Chorus)
There goes sundown
There goes sundown
There goes sundown again

Some days I pray this prayer
More than others
For my Lord to come
When I'm weary of fightin'
When I'm tired of runnin'

Other days I wanna stay around
Grow old with that girl of mine
Most of the future is out of my hands
He reminds me every day about this time

(Repeat Chorus)

(Bridge)
I don't believe we've been forgotten
God's too faithful—he's too good
At keeping all his promises
He's gonna come for me
Just like he said he would

(Repeat Chorus)

Each sundown is a brilliant
reflection of God's perfect
order and timing—a wink
from the Father saying, "I've
not forgotten you . . . peace
be with you."

Know therefore that the Lord your God is God;
he is the faithful God, keeping his covenant of love
to a thousand generations of those who love him
and keep his commands.

Deuteronomy 7:9

ॐ

I'm partial to sundowns. Watching the sun go down from my backyard is one of my favorite things in all the world. Sundown is a built-in, daily signal from God, reminding us of simple, spiritual truths. It reminds me of three spiritual truths in particular—the need for *reflection,* the need for *rest,* and the promise of the Lord's *return.*

When the sun goes down in the evening and the heat of the day begins to subside, my mind naturally turns toward spiritual matters in a moment of *reflection.* We all spend too little time reflecting, too little time alone. Solitude gives me time to consider my walk with the Lord in particular and my life walk in general. Gratitude overwhelms me when I ponder the goodness of God. Even when problems must be addressed and dealt with—when mistakes must be acknowledged, regretted, confessed, and forgiven—even then, thankfulness for God's faithfulness and for all his blessings rises to the top.

Sundown is a good time to call it quits too—a reminder to rest. I continue to be amazed at the energy and work ethic of my wife, Lynn. For all our years together, she's been a wife, a homemaker, and a mom. Her job is never done. Still, I try to encourage her to say, at some point in the day, "That's it. I've done enough for today." Back before electricity or other types of artificial light, people had to quit working at sundown—they had no choice; they couldn't see! Perhaps sundown is God's suggestion that we lay down our work and rest for a while. Just a thought.

Sundown also signals something else to me. It reminds me that God is faithful to his promises and that he will *return* someday to take me home. Growing up, I often heard that Jesus was coming soon, and—I've got to be brutally honest here—that revelation scared me half to death! Beyond being frightened, I was just plain *not excited* about it. I was just beginning to learn about life, and frankly, there were some things I was really looking forward to. I specifically remember praying, and I'm not joking here, "Lord, I know you're coming back soon, but I sure do hope you'll hold off until I get my driver's license!" After the driver's license stage, I prayed, "Lord, it's me again . . . I know you're coming soon, but I sure would like to get married and have a family before the world comes to an end." Life and years continue to present options, and some of them look pretty good, don't they? But I have to say that as the years go by, life's goodies have become less and less attractive. Earth is not our home. For the Christian man, woman, or child, there will always be an unfulfilled longing for the uninterrupted, eternal presence of the Lord.

With each sundown I remember that God has blessed me with one more day, and I pray that he will give me the capacity and the good sense to live each day in a way that will bring a smile to his face, to light my world, to love the wife he gave me, and to never stop looking for his return. Each sundown is a brilliant reflection of God's perfect order and timing—a wink from the Father saying, "I've not forgotten you . . . peace be with you."

When the sun goes down in your backyard tonight, do a little *reflecting,* allow yourself to *rest,* and turn your eyes toward the heavens as you wait for his *return.*

PERSONAL REFLECTIONS

1. What are some things you need to spend time reflecting on?

2. How can reflecting on mistakes and problems remind us of God's faithfulness?

3. Do you tend to be a workaholic, unable to stop working and rest? Where can you go or what can you do to get the rest you need?

4. How do you feel about Christ's return? Do you still feel somewhat tied to the earth? What is holding you here?

life response

Go outside this evening and enjoy sundown. Spend some time in *reflection*, plan for an evening of *rest*, and anticipate the Lord's *return*.

THREE

Would
I
Know
You

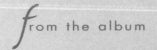

from the album

WATERCOLOUR PONIES

Would I Know You

Would I know you now
If you walked into the room
If you stilled the crowd
If your light dispelled the gloom
And if I saw your wounds
Touched your thorn-pierced brow
I wonder if I'd know you now

Would I know you now
If you walked into this place
Would I cause you shame
Would my games be your disgrace
Or would I worship you
Fall upon my face
I wonder if I'd know you now

Or have the images I've painted
So distorted who you are
That even if the world was looking
They couldn't see you
The real you
Have I changed the true reflection
To fulfill my own design
Making you what I want
Not showing you forth divine

Would I miss you now
If you left and closed the door
Would my flesh cry out,
"I don't need you anymore"
Or would I follow you
Seek to be restored?
I wonder, I wonder
Will I ever learn
I wonder, would I know you now

He's not beyond throwing us an occasional curve just to make sure we're paying attention.

Has not God chosen those who are poor in the eyes
of the world to be rich in faith and to inherit
the kingdom he promised those who love him?
James 2:5

S he walked down the aisle of the church in the middle of the service. Her quiet sobs were mixed with a plea: "Somebody, help me . . . won't somebody please help me?"

An uncomfortable stillness filled the auditorium. People shifted in their seats, straining to see this strange woman with the shameless request: "Won't somebody please help me." We all felt we should *do* something, but no one knew *what* to do. So we just sat there. Nothing like this had ever happened in our church before. The pastor stopped midsentence as the woman made her way up to the platform.

When the pastor finally started talking to her after what seemed like hours, we were all relieved to realize that it had been a setup, a dramatic presentation to make a point about our church body.

There were several points made that day and more than a few questions asked.

As I reflect on how I felt as I watched this loud, unabashed woman walk slowly toward the pulpit, interrupting our "sacred" assembly, I try to pinpoint the root of my discomfort. And as much as I hate to admit it, I think the basis of my uneasiness was the fact that she was behaving *differently*. And different is often translated by our small minds as *undesirable*.

Do you remember the conversation in Mark 9 between Jesus and the disciples? Let me refresh your memory.

> [Jesus] asked them, "What were you arguing about on the road?" But they kept quiet because on the way they had argued about who was the greatest.
>
> Sitting down, Jesus called the Twelve and said, "If anyone wants to be first, he must be the very last, and the servant of all." . . .
>
> "Teacher," said John, "we saw a man driving out demons in your name and we told him to stop, because he was not one of us."
>
> "Do not stop him," Jesus said. "No one who does a miracle in my name can in the next moment say anything bad about me, for whoever is not against us is for us." (Mark 9:33–40)

There are a couple of things going on in this scenario, but *pride* is in the middle of it all. The disciples started out arguing about who among them was the greatest. And the pride rooted there set the stage for their exclusive attitude toward a man who was doing good but was *different* from them. "How snobbish!" we say. But aren't we sometimes guilty of the same thing?

Over the years, God has kept me aware of how easily I'm swayed toward pride over the relationship I have with him. Pride takes many forms. We can be prideful over how long we've known him, over our understanding of Scripture, over what church we attend, and on and on. You get the picture.

Sometimes the prescribed order of our personal walk should take a back seat to the immediate work of the Spirit in our daily living. We can certainly benefit from the knowledge we've gained in years gone by, but there's still a lot to learn today; God is not through with us.

It's difficult not to frame God in some predetermined definition based on what we already know. But we must keep our eyes, our ears, and our hearts open—he just might want to stretch us. As we go through our days with our well-oiled version of faith, I think we'd be wise to remember what Jesus told his disciples: "Whoever is not against us is for us." While God is most certainly a God of order and systems, I'm pretty sure he's not beyond throwing us an occasional curve just to make sure we're paying attention.

If the Lord approached me in what I would consider an extreme form—beggar or rich man, clean-cut or dirty, dressed up or dressed down—would I see him for who he is? Or would I be mindlessly turned off by dirt and poverty and shamefully impressed by upscale wealth?

Look deep into the hearts of those around you today. Look past their outer garments, past their business potential, past their particular church associations, past their exteriors and into their hearts. See them as the Lord sees them. You'll see some saints; you'll see some sinners. You'll see some who are needy and some who almost look like angels. And with the help of spiritual eyes, you'll see a potential spark of God in every one—even in those who are *different.*

⌒

PERSONAL REFLECTIONS

1. Think of someone in your life whom you feel superior to. What can you do to change your attitude?

2. How do you feel when you see a homeless person on the street or someone dressed in dirty, unkempt clothes?

3. Is it possible that your view of God is too narrow? In what areas?

4. Is there someone in your life right now whom God is trying to use to break down your pride?

life response

The next time you see a homeless or conspicuously odd person, see him or her as Jesus would. View the person with respect, and impart dignity to him or her in your heart.

25

FOUR

Almighty

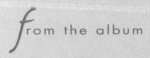

from the album

HOME FREE

Almighty

(Chorus)
Almighty, most Holy God
Faithful through the ages
Almighty, most Holy Lord
Glorious Almighty God

The beasts of the field
The birds of the air
Are silent to call out your name
The earth has no voice
And I have no choice
But to magnify God unashamed

Let the rocks be kept silent for one more day
Let the whole world sing out
Let the people say

(Repeat Chorus)

Time marches on
With innocence gone
And a darkness has covered the earth
But His Spirit still dwells
He speaks "It is well"
And the hopeless still offered new birth

He will break the leash of death
It will have no sting
Let the prisoner go free
Join the dance and sing

(Repeat Chorus)

Instead of
focusing on
the tiny
pebbles in
the road
you travel
today, lift
your eyes to
the Father
and the
promises
that lie at
the end of
the journey.

I will extol the Lord at all times;
his praise will always be on my lips.

Psalm 34:1

⁓

*T*he longer I know the Lord, the more certain I am
that he answers prayer.

But I've also learned that he answers in his own time—
sometimes yes, sometimes no, and sometimes wait. When I
wrote the song "Almighty," I was going through a time when
I was less than happy with my walk with the Lord, and I was
frustrated that my prayers were not being answered the way I
wanted them to be. But God used that time to teach me a lesson I'll never forget. I remember sensing God telling me to
simply *acknowledge* him—to recognize him for who he is and
to allow him to be God in my life and in my circumstances.
He reminded me that he is faithful—that he has been faithful

31

through the ages past, that he is faithful now, and that he will be faithful in times to come.

I don't find it difficult to praise God when things are going good. In fact, things don't really have to be going *good* for me to praise God; they just have to be going the way *I* think they should go!

Sometimes, I manage to praise the Lord when I'm going through difficult times, but while I'm praising God with my mouth, my heart snatches the difficulty from the hands of the Holy Spirit, and I attempt to manipulate the situation— instead of trusting it to his care with a "Your will, not mine, be done." Under these circumstances, my praise can be vain. At other times, I may feel sorry for myself and see myself as one of the "sorely mistreated." I speak in pitiful tones of my sorry situation and then tag my stories with the obligatory, "But I'm praising the Lord anyway."

Am I the only one who struggles with this, or do you also sometimes play tug-of-war with the Holy Spirit or sing the song "Poor, Poor, Pitiful Me"?

A heart that truly praises God, in good times and bad, places the emphasis on *him*—on his power, his wisdom, his discernment, his ability to know what is best for me—not on me and my woeful predicament. A heart of praise is a heart of *trust*—a trust that transcends earthly circumstances.

Sometimes we get bogged down in the trivial details of our daily existence, examining every minuscule element for evidence of God's involvement. Instead of focusing on the tiny pebbles in the road you travel today, lift your eyes to the Father and the promises that lie at the end of the journey.

Remember God's past faithfulness and use those examples to fuel your faith. Trust that he will continue to watch over you and love you with an everlasting love.

PERSONAL REFLECTIONS

1. How can simply acknowledging God increase our trust in him?

2. Think of a time when, instead of trusting a difficulty to God, you tried to take matters into your own hands. What happened? What would you do differently if you had it to do over again?

3. How does self-pity inhibit praise? Have you ever allowed self-pity to interfere with trusting God?

4. What minuscule details in your life have you been focusing on when you should have been focusing on God? Lift up your eyes.

life response

Praise God for a difficulty in your life; thank him that you can always trust him to work his perfect will in your life.

FIVE

Material Magic

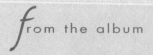

*f*rom the album

WATERCOLOUR PONIES

Material Magic

Pressure's on—I can't slow down
Gotta make it—'fore my best years pass me by
Up before dawn—building my crown
In my own eyes it's a noble sacrifice

I spend my time
Tryin' to make a little hay
Before the sun stops shinin'

Material magic
Got a spell on me
One more time

Pile it high
Save it up for a rainy day
For surprises—unexpected tragedy
Funny thing is
It can all blow away
Leave ya broken, leave ya beggin'
Down on your knees

36

It makes good sense
Till the walls of my security
Come crashin' in

Material magic
Got a spell on me
One more time

And the checkbooks
And the credit cards go flyin'
You can get 'em in the mail
Before you apply
Can my limit take the weight of what I'm buyin'?
Good money down on my own slice of the pie

Are we crazy
Or just out of control
That we bow down to what money can buy?
Seems like people will trade in their souls
For the pleasure—for the ecstasy of the eye

But does Jesus weep
That I spend my time collectin'
What I cannot keep?
I heard him say
Lay your treasure up
Where the hands of time
Cannot decay

Material magic
Got a spell on me
One more time

37

THIS NOTE IS LE
R ALL DEBTS, PUB

"Sometimes more
isn't better . . .
sometimes it's just more."

I know what it is to be in need,
and I know what it is to have plenty.
I have learned the secret of being content in any and
every situation, whether well fed or hungry,
whether living in plenty or in want.
Philippians 4:12

To say that Lynn and I had "nothing" when we married would be an exaggeration. To say that what we had was simple and that our possessions were few and far between is more accurate—but even that description is relative.

I remember our first apartment in college. We were happy just to be married and to be on our own. Our few pieces of furniture meant little, if anything, to us. Our needs and wants were simple, and our eyes seldom scanned the landscape of the world's stuff—our eyes were constantly fixed on each other.

When we left school and moved into the working world, we quickly outgrew apartment number two and moved into

apartment number three—just down the sidewalk, but a little bigger to accomodate our firstborn, Neal. Still, most
things were out of our reach financially, and we were content.

But as the years passed, our focus gradually shifted. We
occasionally allowed our eyes to move off each other and
God and increasingly linger on the "things" in our view. I
remember little snapshots of our family and the changes we
made. Our first house was *perfect* . . . or was it? Wouldn't it
be good to have a chair in that corner? And wouldn't this
room look better painted another color? What color? Oh, it
doesn't matter—as long as it's different. And, ya know, I've
been thinking, this kitchen would be *just right* if the wall
were just a few more feet out that way. Wouldn't that be
great?

You get the picture. You may have one or two such mental
images of your own. Wanting more can become a dangerous
snowball that is difficult, if not impossible, to stop. Once you
paint the walls, the floor looks bad. And if you touch up the
floor, the old furniture will need to find a new home.

As I write these words, my twenty-fourth anniversary
approaches, and I can say without reservation, but with some
embarrassment, that over the years, material possessions have
caused about as many problems in our marriage as anything I
can think of.

I've come to realize that this disease of *wanting more* is a
device of Satan. When you feel it, know that Satan is at work,
setting up those material gadgets as idols in your heart. Those
shiny new acquisitions that clamor for your attention can
subtly move into the position in your heart that rightly

belongs to the Lord. Living disciplined lives, when it comes to finances, is one of life's great challenges, for money can be deceptive, and even cruel.

But money in and of itself is not the problem. It's the *love* of money that gets us in trouble. It's sadly amusing to hear people "quote" 1 Timothy 6:10 and say: "Money is the root of all evil." They may think they're quoting Scripture, but look again. What the passage really says is "The *love* of money is a root of all kinds of evil." It's not money that's evil; it's our love of it, our wholehearted pursuit of it, that's wrong.

Money used for good blesses many. I thank God for the people of material wealth who have given to countless good works around the world and throughout history. Giving pleases the Lord. Remember the story of Jesus and the woman who gave just a few cents at the temple? Christ was more impressed by the sacrifice of this dear lady than with other larger gifts that day. Whether from our wealth or from our want, giving demonstrates that we are more interested in seeing his purpose accomplished than in accumulating more for ourselves. The noble and honorable management of the material assets God has given us pleases the Giver of all we have.

There was a wonderful movie re-make in the mid-nineties called *Sabrina.* Sabrina was the simple but beautiful daughter of a chauffeur who worked for a wealthy, successful (in one sense of the word) businessman. Sabrina grew up appreciating the beautiful things that she saw from afar, but also appreciating the simple, quiet life her father lived.

As she grew into a young woman, her fascination with the wealthy businessman grew into infatuation and finally love.

41

Sabrina found, however, that she was distressed over his pursuit of "more." In one unforgettable line, Sabrina declared, "Sometimes more isn't better . . . sometimes it's just more."

Carefully evaluate your desires for more. I'm certain that God wants us to enjoy the life he gives us here on earth, but I know we break his heart when we let our eyes wander toward things that are rusting and decaying even before we possess them!

Possessions can be very demanding, but we can choose to take control. We can deny possessions their power by keeping them off the throne of our heart. Take care that your possessions serve you—and not the other way around—as you serve *him*.

PERSONAL REFLECTIONS

1. Have you become less content as you have gained more?

2. What things in your life make you feel discontent? What can you do to find contentment in those areas?

3. How does Satan use discontentment to pull us to him?

4. What's the difference in *loving* money and *having* money? Why is one okay and the other not?

5. Do you have any possessions that you find yourself serving, instead of making them serve you?

life response

The cure for discontentment is thankfulness. Consider things in your life that you are not content with and find ways to thank God— even for the items of discontent. Remember: Happiness is not getting what you want but being happy with what you've got.

SIX

When God's People Pray

*f*rom the album

HOME FREE

When God's People Pray

Trouble knocking on your window pane
Stormy weather at your door
And the outlook for the day ahead
Like the day before

People tell ya praying changes things
But words don't stop the fear
A prayer is only pious rambling
Without a Father's ear

He will not turn away
When his people pray

(Chorus)
When God's people pray
And take the pains of earth
To the doors of heaven

When God's people pray
There is hope reborn
There is sin forgiven
And miracles you can't explain away
When God's people pray

Hopeless situation turns around
Dilemma passes by and by
Look, there's a never ending field of blue
Past your clouded sky

He alone can know the need in me
Before a single word begins
The Holy Spirit intercedes for me
I will trust in him

He will not turn away
When his people pray

(Repeat Chorus)

God, help us to
approach you
without the slightest
fear, knowing that
your ways and your
love are perfect.

This is the confidence we have in approaching God:
that if we ask anything according to his will,
he hears us. And if we know that he hears us—
whatever we ask—we know that we have
what we asked of him.

1 John 5:14–15

ॐ

Maybe I'm making too much out of this—it wouldn't be the first time I've been accused of putting something under a critical microscope—but the bumper-sticker slogan "Prayer Changes Things" has really set me to thinking. I don't want to be overly analytical, but God gave us brains, and I figure he intends that we use them. From what I hear, most of us don't tap even a small percentage of our brains' capabilities, so let's crank up the gray matter!

I hope you'll pay attention here, because what I'm about to say could be totally misunderstood: Prayer doesn't change anything. Yes, you heard me right. *Prayer* doesn't change things; *God* changes things. Like I said, this could be considered hair splitting or gnat killing, but I think it's important to remember that God is the only divine one in the prayer equation. Too often, the fact that the Father does hear our prayers and always answers them (whether we realize it or not) spawns some vanity on the part of us mortals. It can lead to a place of spiritual pride. When viewed outside of a spiritual perspective, answered prayers might lead us to believe that we can manipulate God to do our bidding. This view of the relationship between the created and the Creator is totally without basis. It's true that the Bible says that "the prayer of a righteous man is powerful and effective" (James 5:16). But let's not forget that it is God who makes things happen when we pray, not us.

Answered prayer should bring us to our knees. I don't know if it should overwhelm or surprise us, because, frankly, as we grow in Christ and in an intimate relationship with him, we should expect our prayers to be heard and answered. But I don't want to ever take God's ears for granted. I don't want to ever be so casual with the heavenly Father that I grow complacent in my faith. There is a fine line between comfort in the presence of our loving Father and prideful apathy.

Scripture says that we may "approach the throne of grace with boldness" (Heb. 4:16 NRSV). One of the biggest challenges in the life of any believer is learning how to come boldly before our loving Father without arrogance and pride.

God, help us remove any thoughts of manipulating heaven with our prayers. God, help us learn to approach you with complete assurance and trust and without the slightest fear, knowing that your ways and your love are perfect.

PERSONAL REFLECTIONS

1. Why is it important to make the distinction between "Prayer changes things" and "God changes things"?

2. How can a prayer answered as we requested tempt us to think that we can manipulate God?

3. Recall a prayer that God answered as you wanted him to. Recall one he answered differently than you'd hoped. How does faith in God allow you to accept both answers?

4. Have you ever crossed over the line between comfort with your heavenly Father and arrogant demands? Ask God to forgive you and humble your heart as you pray.

life response

Practice approaching God with the proper balance of comfortable confidence and absolute humility. Ask him for help in achieving this balance.

SEVEN

Water-colour Ponies

Watercolour Ponies

There are watercolour ponies
On my refrigerator door
And the shape of something I don't really recognize
Brushed with careful little fingers
And put proudly on display
A reminder to us all of how time flies

Seems an endless mound of laundry
And a stairway laced with toys
Give a blow-by-blow reminder of the war
That we fight for their well-being
For their greater understanding
To impart a holy reverence for the Lord

(Chorus)
But baby, what will we do
When it comes back to me and you?

They look a little less like little boys every day
Oh, the pleasure of watchin' the children growin'
Is mixed with a bitter cup
Of knowin' the watercolour ponies
Will one day ride away

And the vision can get so narrow
As you view thru your tiny world
And little victories go by with no applause
But in the greater evaluation
As they fly from your nest of love
May they mount up with wings as eagles for his cause

(Repeat Chorus)

*Children won't wait until we arrive
in our faith to observe our lives;
they are watching our journey.*

Children are a gift from the Lord; babies are a reward.
Children who are born to a young man
are like arrows in the hand of a warrior.
Happy is the man who has a bag full of arrows.
They will not be defeated when they fight their enemies
at the city gate.

Psalm 127:3 NCV

The hands of the clock continue their movement undaunted. They aren't threatened by my deadlines, and they know nothing of what I count important. The moments marked by their progression are made up of seemingly insignificant, mundane events.

But ordinary, day-to-day occurrences often have tremendous impact on our children. Children are like little video cameras on legs, recording on their hearts all that they see in our lives. And our "mundane" lives are the prime subject of their movies. What they see in us affects who they turn out to be.

Those of us who are Christian parents want our children to follow *Jesus,* but the truth is, folks, in those early years, they will follow *us.* We are the first Jesus our children see. We can't think that pointing our children toward Jesus exonerates us from living a godly example before them. Being faithful in small, everyday events speaks volumes to our children and is a testimony of the living Christ. They won't wait until we *arrive* in our faith to observe our lives; they are watching our *journey.*

And we're doing it, aren't we? We're winning victories in the quiet, everyday realm of our lives—pursuing godliness without fanfare or parade. Many of us receive little, if any, applause—except for (as Max Lucado puts it) the *applause of heaven!* But we persevere in our journey, we continue to fight the battles, we persist in offering our services to him—whether celebrated by others or offered in secret—all because our hearts' desire is to do all things as unto the Lord (Col. 3:23).

One specific I feel compelled to mention is the image we give our children of our day-to-day relationship with our spouses. They watch how we treat one another and are aware of our love—or lack of it. I believe children need to know that our spouses are our *first love* under heaven. Too many parents devote every waking moment pouring over their children, meeting their needs, and assuring them they are loved—to the neglect of their husband or wife. Now, don't get me wrong. Demonstrating love to our children is a high priority, but demonstrating love for our spouse is an even greater priority. It's critical that children know (even though it might be somewhat disturbing at first) that Mom and Dad are first with each other and that only God takes a higher place in their hearts.

The security imparted to a child through observing a solid display of love, affection, and friendship between parents is immeasurable! The ladder of love in a home is an important representation of the order of authority in their lives. When their little worlds shake and fall apart, they will find comfort in our solid love for each other. God finds many ways of dispensing his peace to his children—our love for our mates is one of his dispensers.

Your house may be a little more cluttered than you would like, and you probably don't have as much time for yourself as you desire, but remember—these years are quickly passing. One phase of childhood moves swiftly and unannounced into the next. Thank God today for his blessing of children. Embrace every moment—whether happy, sad, or stressful. In every snapshot of the journey lies a life lesson that is worth learning.

PERSONAL REFLECTIONS

1. If you are a parent, what "mundane" event did your child observe in you today that might have an eternal impact?

2. If your children follow you, what will be their destination?

3. Name a specific victory you recently won or a service you offered that was witnessed by your child.

4. Why is the love between a husband and wife of greater priority than their love for their children? How do you demonstrate love to your spouse in view of your child?

5. How does loving your spouse offer security to your child?

life response

See your child today as a video camera on legs and do something specific that will create a lasting impression for good on his or her heart.

EIGHT

God in a Box

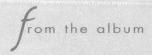
A BEAUTIFUL PLACE

God in a Box

Down on the corner
They've got it all figured out
Little room for mystery
Little room for doubt
Got no time for questions
Everything is black and white

A little further down the highway
They're studyin' the Word,
"If you ain't heard our version, brother,
You ain't really heard
It's our darlin' revelation
Everything is crystal clear"

Cool and collected
Nothin' left to learn
Nearly perfected

Lord have mercy on our arrogant souls
Before we were us
It was you alone, I know

(Chorus)
God ain't gonna stay
In the little box I put him in
He won't be contained by
Some shiny, wrapped-up view of him
God ain't gonna stay
In the little box I put him in

Lord, we know everything you're up to
Know just what to expect
Who you're gonna nail
And who you're gonna protect
So come on, line 'em up
All our little ducks in a row

(Bridge)
Who's got all the answers
God is no puppet on a string
He ain't no carnival prancer
Open up the doors for the strong and mighty king

(Repeat Chorus)

(Repeat Bridge)

(Repeat Chorus)

We have succeeded in removing the veil of mystery from the Almighty and have proudly declared God "known."

Then the Lord answered Job out of the storm.
He said: "Who is this that darkens my counsel
with words without knowledge? Brace yourself like a man;
I will question you, and you shall answer me.
Where were you when I laid the earth's foundation?
Tell me, if you understand."

Job 38:1–4

᠌᠊

*I*t wasn't supposed to turn out this way. All those years of regular church attendance were never intended to lead us here; but here we are, and we find that our destination is very much our own making.

God has been found out—completely understood and put on display for all to see. It's almost as if we view God as just another trophy, a product representing some great human accomplishment: "Here are my medals for perfect Sunday school attendance—five years! And over here is my little league state championship trophy, and if you'll look right this way, you'll see God."

Pardon me if I lump us all together for a minute or two—feel free to excuse or exclude yourself if you wish—*we have robbed God of his mystery.* Now obviously, I'm not implying that any one of us has the power to take anything from God that he doesn't allow us to take, but as members of this "all-aware" and somewhat arrogant generation, we have succeeded in removing the veil of mystery from the Almighty and have proudly declared God "known."

Some of us have been studying Scripture all our lives. That's good! But when we take Scripture out of its eternal context and reduce it to a set of rules, we become filled with a kind of unholy arrogance. More than a few times, I've thought to myself, *Okay, I've done step one, step two, and step three; I've gone by all the rules and followed the orders—now God has to do what I ask.*

Can you see how this attitude humanizes God in a way that strips him of his majesty, his deity? What vanity to expect the creator of the universe to be subservient to our rules and demands!

While much of the believer's life is spent in pursuit of knowing *about* God, perhaps more time should be spent seeking to know *him.* Rather than idolizing *knowledge,* we need to learn to trust him with what little we do know and with all that we don't know. While living out what we know from his Word, we must always leave room for the unseen, unexplainable, humanly unfathomable mysteries of God. Sure, this approach might take us humans down a couple of notches, but it will humble us and remind us that we are only clay in the Potter's hands.

PERSONAL REFLECTIONS

1. What limits have you put on God that Scripture does not?

2. How do our definitions of God strip him of his majesty?

3. What is the difference in seeking to know *God* and seeking to know *about* God?

life response

Meditate on the greatness of God—in creation, in Scripture, in you. Seek to knock down the walls of your box.

NINE

It's Time

It's Time

It happened many years ago
The memories still haunt you though
And who's to blame? You really don't know
You're just locked all alone in these chains

Sometimes it's hard to live at all
The pictures of your history call
Your mind's a decorated wall
But the Lord has the cure for your pain

(Chorus)
It's time, come back to the land of the living
Come home to the land of forgiving
Jesus will be faithful to the end
It's time, break the tangled webs that bind you
Let the grace of God unwind you

Give the Lord your broken heart to mend
It's time . . . it's time

You've had your little victories
But perfection's pretty hard to please
And guilt is an annoying breeze
That blows all that's peaceful away

And your life is too short
To go on living like this
Or to brood over who's done you wrong
If the years pass you by
Look at all that you'll miss
You've been walking in shadows too long

(Repeat Chorus)

IT'S TIME by Wayne Watson
© 1992 Word Music (A Div. of WORD MUSIC) and Material Music (Admin. by WORD MUSIC).
All Rights Reserved. Used By Permission.

The sooner you and I begin to clean out the filthy rags that fill our bags, the sooner we will walk with a lighter step and a more joyful heart.

Therefore, since we are surrounded
by such a great cloud of witnesses,
let us throw off everything that hinders
and the sin that so easily entangles,
and let us run with perseverance
the race marked out for us.

Hebrews 12:1

Emotional baggage is one of Satan's most effective weapons against humanity. I can think of few things that are as detrimental to our walk with God than emotional baggage —and Satan has an entire product line. Let's see, there are those oversized suitcases that, when full, can barely be lifted, much less carried for any distance. These huge bags can hold a lifetime of hurt—childhood abuse and neglect, marital bitterness and betrayal, failed friendships, broken business relationships—real hurts, deep pain. A bag this size can nearly incapacitate the person who is burdened with it.

Then there are the mid-size suitcases that come equipped with wheels so you can roll your emotional weight behind you. These bags are just the right size for storing the oppressive weight of guilt, memories of past failures, and wounds inflicted by our personal limitations—you know, limitations like physical handicaps, personality quirks, financial difficulties, and a whole list of natural imperfections. Some of the distress we feel in carrying these bags is self-inflicted, as we belittle ourselves for our imperfections, and some is caused by those around us. These emotional hurts fit nicely into the mid-size bag and can be lugged just about anywhere.

Backpacks are a convenient way to carry grudges and hurt feelings. Thoughtless words, intentional snubbings, accidental oversights, inconsiderations of all sizes—all can be carted in this compact bag. We can even stop every now and then, take the articles of hurt out, turn them over, remember just when they happened, and relive the pain of each incident—reinforcing our dislike of the one who inflicted the pain. Backpacks are just right for carrying the little hurts we want to remember often.

Satan knew what he was doing when he developed emotional baggage. It's always with us, it hinders our walk, it reminds us of our pain, and although it can be very heavy and difficult to maintain, it becomes a part of our very being.

In truth, we all carry emotional baggage of some sort. None of us are totally free of it; none of us are unmarred by pain, hurtful memories, or the guilt of sin. Each of us has a secret or two that would startle or at least disappoint those we know. Too many times, we store our hurts away in our bags, intending to deal with them later. Hidden from sight, they are easy to forget. Out of sight, out of mind. Early memories of sin might be hidden under more recent garments of failure, but they're still there—haunting us.

But it's time to deal with the whole collection. Right now. I'm not so naive as to think that a lifetime of guilt and secrets and hurts can be vanquished in a moment—although I'm absolutely certain that if God wanted to deal with your issues that way, he could. But you *can* start simply. Some of the unpacking will be painful and traumatic, but the sooner you and I begin to clean out the filthy rags that fill our bags, the sooner we will walk with a lighter step and a more joyful heart.

Some will need to seek professional help or the help of a pastor or church counselor. Please do. If some tears need to flow, let them. Know that the loving arms of God are patiently waiting to welcome you into a more perfect fellowship. I believe that the Father grieves with us over the burdensome baggage that hinders our race. God and all of heaven are cheering for you.

PERSONAL REFLECTIONS

1. What memories of past hurt or guilt does Satan use to haunt you?

2. How do past hurts and painful memories hinder our walk with God?

3. How is it harmful to keep hurts stuffed away in emotional bags and not deal with them?

life response

Open up one of your bags today. Take out one item and bring it to the throne of God in prayer. Ask God to heal your heart concerning this matter.

TEN

Child
of
Beth-
lehem

Child of Bethlehem

Still quiet night in Bethlehem
Earth sleeps and few take thought of him
But the heavens rejoice
And the angels sing
The Child of Bethlehem is the King of Kings

Still, wise men worship at his feet
And lost souls awaken from their sleep
And the heavens rejoice
And the angels sing
The Child of Bethlehem is the King of Kings

Down from heaven's glory
To a manger bed
Crucified, glorified
He was born to be our Savior

Come children over all the earth
Come celebrate the Savior's birth
Every knee shall bow
And every nation sing
The Child of Bethlehem is the King of Kings

Come children over all the earth
Come celebrate the Savior's birth
Every knee shall bow
And every nation sing
The Child of Bethlehem is the King of Kings
The Child of Bethlehem is the King of Kings

When he speaks, stop what you're
doing, hush your conversation,
and hang on his every word.

*If anyone has ears to hear,
let him hear.*
Mark 4:23

୬

Lynn and I took our first trip to Israel in late summer, 1996. It was an awesome experience. Places that had previously been only words on a page came to life right in front of me. Sitting on the Mount of Olives, praying in the Garden of Gethsemane, walking up the Via Dolorosa—all these experiences had a profound effect on my understanding of what my Lord went through for me.

With all the wonderful sights, one of my most poignant experiences was extremely simple. Out on a little boat on the Sea of Galilee, I began to imagine a normal day in the life of Jesus. As a child, reading about Christ and his life through years of Sunday school, I envisioned his every experience as momentous. I think I imagined Christ like the man in the old E. F. Hutton TV commercials. You remember the scene: A roomful of people are talking in groups of two or three, and the noise of their conversations blends into a blurred sound, no voice rising above another. Until . . . one particular man speaks and *everyone* in the room stops his or her conversation and turns to listen to this "wise" man. And you hear the announcer say, "When E. F. Hutton speaks, people listen!"

Well, that's how I saw Jesus. I imagined that everywhere he went, people immediately stopped their work, hushed their conversations, and focused their attention on him.

But out on that little boat, it occured to me that my childhood vision was a little off. This was a busy place, filled with people who, much like people today, were set on their own courses and busy with their own purposes. And Jesus was an ordinary looking man. Most of them probably never stopped to listen to Jesus and hear what he had to say. Most had probably heard the rumors and read the tabloids about some strange preacher in their community but were just too busy to pay attention. He walked down the streets and spoke in the marketplaces unnoticed by the preoccupied masses.

But there were some who had spiritual eyes and ears, who saw him for who he was and heard the power in his words; these people did stop in their paths and hang on his every word. They knew, just as all heaven knew, that this was a unique and spectacular time in history. Wise men and women still recognize his majesty today.

Draw away from the insignificant and distracting matters of your day, and tune your ear to hear the voice of the Lord.

Meditate on the awesome wonder of our Savior. His power and wisdom and his abiding love are as real today as they were when he walked this earth two thousand years ago—heeded by a few and overlooked by many. When he speaks, stop what you're doing, hush your conversation, and hang on his every word.

PERSONAL REFLECTIONS

1. Do you think you would have recognized Jesus for who he was if you lived in Israel while he walked this earth?

2. What does it mean to have "ears to hear"?

3. How was Jesus ordinary and indistinguishable from the crowd?

4. How was Jesus absolutely different from every other person who's ever lived?

life response

Spend some time today reading some of the words of Jesus. Try to hear them with fresh ears, as if hearing them for the first time.

ELEVEN

The Fine Line

The Fine Line

There's a fine line
Between contentment and greed
Between the things that I want
And the things that I need
Between "enough is enough"
And where desires feed
It's a fine line

How do I live with so much
Here with the spoil of the blessed
And not abandon this boat
For the sea of excess?
To aspire to great things
Yet be filled with humbleness
It's a fine line—oh yes, it's a fine line

(Chorus)
So where do I walk, where is my place?

86

The straight and the narrow
The road of grace
Holdin' fast to you, walkin' at your pace
Walkin' on the fine line
Walkin, on the fine line
Walkin, on the fine line

There's a fine line
Between taking bread with a lost man
And being consumed by his way
While reaching out in love
Temptation's right at your door
Guard what you're thinking of
It's a fine line

When I hide my eyes
From the darkest of our life's insanity
From the worst of the world's profanity
I've gotta be careful
I don't miss anyone in need of me
It's a fine line
Oh yes, it's a fine line

And can I embrace the world's sorrow
And not be carried away by life's rain
Know the power of the resurrection
And still know the fellowship of his pain?
Not talkin' 'bout walkin' fences
Not talkin' 'bout compromise
But living and breathing as pleasing in his eyes

(Repeat Chorus)

Walking the
fine line . . .

. . . doesn't mean
riding the fence.

The spiritual man makes judgments
about all things, but he himself
is not subject to any man's judgment.

1 Corinthians 2:15

o you sometimes find it difficult to live separate from
the world yet not isolated from it? There's a fine line between
reaching out to those who live in the darkness and being
pulled into the darkness with them.

As we try to reflect the image of Christ to the world, many
decisions are easy. Few would argue that abusing ourselves
with harmful chemicals is permissible. The Scriptures are clear
about sexual sin. And "thou shalt not steal" is a definite scriptural instruction. The list is long. "Big sins" are usually easy to
identify and steer clear of—if we so choose.

But not everything is black and white. Some areas are separated only by a fine line, and these lines can vary from culture

to culture or even church to church. Who can discern where these fine lines begin and end? You and I! We are not left alone.

Armed with scriptural truth and the promises of God and led by the Spirit, you and I can fight against the darkness without being consumed by it. The Lord gives us insight on how to use every opportunity without compromise. I've never felt abandoned by God for doing what I really felt compelled to do, *out of obedience.* During those times I always feel his guiding presence.

Walking the fine line doesn't mean riding the fence, and knowing how far you can reach into the world with the compassion of the Lord without being pulled down by its filth and the traps is not always easy. The limits we set depend on motive, spiritual maturity, and readiness. If the motive is love for the lost world, the chances dimish that we'll wander off course. The surest way to avoid being sucked into the darkness is to remain securely harnessed to the Christ.

Many Christians worry (or should we use the more spiritually-correct term, *are concerned?*) that associating with those in the darkness in order to reach them for Christ will affect their reputations. There's that fine line again. Where is the fine line between forging ahead—led by the Spirit, not worrying about others think—and legitimate concern for our reputations? We *must* keep our distance from evil and temptation, but isn't it a bit selfish and arrogant to refuse to step into the darkness to save the lost just because we're concerned for our reputations? Where is our faith?

The balance is delicate. But God is gracious in providing not only the plan, but also the Spirit as our leader and guide. When, indeed, the line is fine, God is our divine balancing pole.

PERSONAL REFLECTIONS

1. Think of a specific situation when you had to discern the fine line between associating with the world in order to share Christ and keeping yourself spotless from the world. What did you do? Would you do anything different if you had it to do over again? What?

2. What's the difference in walking the fine line and riding the fence?

3. What does this mean: "The surest way to avoid being sucked into the darkness is to remain securely harnessed to the Christ"?

4. Have you ever been in a situation where reaching out to a lost or hurting person put your reputation under fire?

life response

Take inventory of those in your realm of influence. Find someone in the world who needs the touch of Christ and make it a point to touch that person.

TWELVE

By
Any
Other
Name

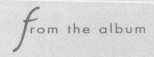

*f*rom the album

FIELD OF SOULS

By Any Other Name

At the name all heaven fell at his feet
At the name the saving of the world was done
On the lips of everyone
Wanting God's complete forgiveness
Every soul in desperation
Everybody in pain
Every broken heart can call on the name

(Chorus)
His name is Jesus
And I am not ashamed
To call on Jesus
Heaven's door will not be opened
By any other name

To the name, the world has grown so cold
As if eternal life could just be bought and sold

As if the precious blood of Christ
Was spilled for no good reason
But every knee will bow one day
And every tongue will proclaim
That the perfect son of heaven
Is the name above all names

(Repeat Chorus)

And here on earth some call it out in vile profanity
And take the name of Christ in vain
Life in the world has robbed some innocence away from me
Through it all I know he loves me
I will glorify the name

(Repeat Chorus)

BY ANY OTHER NAME by Wayne Watson
© 1995 Word Music (A Div. of WORD MUSIC) and Material Music (Admin. by WORD MUSIC).
All Rights Reserved. Used By Permission.

Our meager attempts at "niceness" were no consolation for our Savior as he hung on the Cross, crushed under the mammoth weight of a lost and confused world.

Yet to all who received him,
to those who believed in his name,
he gave the right to become children of God.

John 1:12

᠅

A rose by any other name would still smell as sweet,"
Shakespeare proclaimed. While there is truth in this well-known maxim, some names do make a difference—conjuring up distinct emotions and associations. The name Hitler fills us with disgust and sorrow, while Mother Teresa calls up images of sacrificial love and compassion.

And the name Jesus, the sweetest name of all, is fixed in the minds of all believers as the one who gave himself for our sin. The *name* is forever linked with the *deed*.

> God made his name greater than every other name
> so that every knee will bow to the name of Jesus—

everyone in heaven, on earth, and under the earth. And everyone will confess that Jesus Christ is Lord and bring glory to God the Father.

(Phil. 2:9–11 NCV)

I don't know about you, but hearing the name of Jesus spoken with anything but *respect* makes my skin crawl. And when it's used in casual profanity, my heart hurts, and I feel compelled to whisper an apology to the Lord. The one named *Jesus* is the one who died for me; he gave his life because of *my* sin.

"What do you think being a Christian means?" I asked one of my dinner companions. We were in New York, and several of us had been together all day shooting the cover of my album. We'd gotten to know each other enough to be fairly comfortable—at least comfortable enough to have a good conversation—and the question was not awkward or out of place. But I'll never forget the answer: "Just someone who's a nice person." I was speechless. After a moment of quiet while the words sunk in, we calmly discussed and debated.

As I reflected on those words, "just a nice person," my heart was heavy. Not only for the person who had spoken them, but for the millions of others who embrace such a casual definition of the faith I hold so dear. If I'd ever felt just a bit of the weight of sin and lostness, I felt it then. *Sin* took my Savior to the Cross. No amount of "niceness" can pay for my sin; only the painfully shed blood of a perfect sacrifice could do that. Our meager attempts at "niceness" were no consolation for our Savior as he hung on the cross, crushed under the mammoth weight of a lost and confused world.

Many of your friends, family, coworkers, and schoolmates also define the Christian faith in careless terms such as "being nice." They may never actually put their definition in so many words, but they're *depending* on their niceness to bring them into favor with the heavenly Father. The fourteenth chapter of John's gospel makes it crystal clear that the *only* way to the Father is through the Son, the one given the name above all names.

Jesus never indicated that we could come to the Father by being good, by being American, by being faithful to our spouse, by loving our children, by paying our taxes, and so on. You get the idea.

Let me encourage you to make your own list. Write down things you might count on to bring you into favor with God—things you might feel would improve your chances of "getting into heaven," as I've heard some say—as if we, by our efforts can get ourselves there.

Some folks have this distorted picture of God standing at the door of the kingdom saying, "I'm not supposed to make exceptions, but I've been watching you, and you've been a pretty nice person. So, I'll let you in—but for crying out loud, don't tell anybody!"

As you list those things you're inclined to be proud of, remind yourself of the words of our Lord, "I am the way, and the truth, and the life; no one comes to the Father, *but by me*" (John 14:6 RSV).

PERSONAL REFLECTIONS

1. How do you feel when you hear others use Jesus' name profanely?

2. Why is the definition "nice person" not an accurate description of a Christian?

3. What things are you tempted to count on to bring you into favor with God?

4. What are some specific things you can do to bring honor to the name of Jesus?

life response

If you haven't already done so, write down a list of things you might count on to bring you into favor with God. Contemplate the seriousness of your sin and the heavy price Jesus paid for it. Draw a huge cross over your list—the Cross of Christ is the only thing that can bring you into favor with God.

THIRTEEN

A Season in Your Path

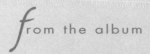

A Season in Your Path

Heard that friends are friends forever
But we don't talk much any more
I guess that I've gone my way
And I guess that you've gone yours

Was kindness too neglected
On my list of deep regret
In spite of distance unexpected
Can we forgive but not forget?

(Chorus)
Sometimes I think about you
Some old memories make me cry
Remembering the good times makes me laugh
But all in all I'm richer for the happy and the sad
And thankful for a season in your path

I guess God alone deciphers
When people need each other most
Who will be the blessed receiver
Who will be the gracious host

And all a servant here can do
Is unto the Lord avail
Content at times to be the wind
And at times to be the sail

If another winter settles
On your shoulder down the road
Without a thought of what's behind us
Let me help you pull your load

(Repeat Chorus)

God pairs people as friends
at the right time and
place and season of need.

As iron sharpens iron,
so one man sharpens another.
Proverbs 27:17

ou and I are products of all the people God has put in our paths—good relationships and bad, infamous acquaintances and inspirational living examples, distant relatives and close friends.

Friendships are blessings from God. There are few among us who don't welcome the sound of a friend's voice in times of trouble. A wise, compassionate, and understanding friend knows when to speak and when to listen and say nothing at all.

Do you remember the story of Job? When his world literally fell apart, his "friends" came to be with him. Most would agree that these friends were more anxious to offer their opinions on why Job's life was in such bad shape than they were to comfort and encourage him. We can all learn a lesson from this story about what kind of friends we should and should not be.

The best friendships involve people who are mutually and intensely interested in each other's welfare. Such friendships are gifts from God. We can do little to make them happen, but we can do a lot to maintain them. Some of my conversations with my closest friends become almost comical at times as each of us tries to move the conversation away from ourselves and onto the other: "That's enough about me. How are you doing?" "No, I don't want to talk about me; I want to know about *you.*" But most casual relationships follow another conversational path: "That's enough about me. Let's talk about you. What do you think of *me?*"

Through the course of your life, friends, close and otherwise, will come and go. Some will move away, and others will just drift away from the intimacy you once shared. Maybe you feel resentful that they aren't as close to you as they used to be; maybe you simply miss them. May I suggest that when you feel alone, sorry for yourself, or neglected that you reflect on the dear people God has placed in your path. One of the most soothing balms for bitter feelings is *gratitude*. Give thanks to the Father for friends in your past. God pairs people as friends at the right time and place and season of need.

Thank him. There will be others who act as emissaries from God down the road. Be grateful. Thanksgiving will dispel feelings of anger and self-pity and will prepare the way for *this* day's blessing from the Lord.

PERSONAL REFLECTIONS

1. What friends have influenced you greatly? How have they influenced you for good or bad?

2. Whom have you been a blessing to as a friend?

3. What friend has drifted out of your life? Are you resentful about this loss? What can you do to dispel that resentment?

life response

Reminisce today. Think of a friend to whom you can say, "I'm thankful for a season in your path."

FOURTEEN

Wouldn't That Be Somethin'

Wouldn't That Be Somethin'

I had this dream and you were in it
There was this party and you were there
Simple evening with just a few close friends
People were pressing for your attention
You were patient, everybody could see
But all the time you were looking 'round the room for me
But hey, after all it's my dream

(Chorus)
I wanna be the kind of friend Jesus would call
Yeah, you know, if he had a telephone
At the end of the day
Just to talk about nothin', nothin'
Yeah, I wanna be the kind of friend he'd wanna be around
You know, without a word, without a sound
Wouldn't that be somethin', somethin', yeah

110

Is that so hard to imagine
The Lord Jesus as a friend like that?
Spending time in the pleasure of your company
True companion like no other
You never had a friend like that
If you're havin' a little trouble believing
Come on, put yourself in my dream

(Repeat Chorus)

Wouldn't that be somethin'
Somethin', yeah

Wouldn't it be something if he walked where we walked? Wouldn't it be something if he could actually be a friend?

I no longer call you servants,
because a servant does not know his master's business.
Instead, I have called you friends.
John 15:15

ↄ

I

t was no one's fault in particular. I grew in a wonderful home where the Lord was worshiped, prayed to, and revered. The things of God permeated every aspect of our small-town lives. The church was not only the center of our spiritual lives, but the headquarters for most of our social activities. The week revolved around what was going on "down at the church." Where I came from, if you weren't in church on Sunday, you didn't go out. You wouldn't want anyone to *know* you weren't in church! The only kind of sickness that constituted an excused absence from Sunday school was one that put you on your back in bed. Some people say, "We were in church every time the doors were open." Hey, we had keys!

But even with this richly spiritual upbringing, some of my earliest images of God were not good. In spite of all the good teaching (I can still remember some of my Sunday school teachers and pals), fellowship, and memories, my strongest mental pictures of the Lord were less than positive.

Two images were indelibly impressed on my mind. The first was of God sitting in this big chair. We're talking about the classic rendition. You've seen the paintings. You know, the Michelangelo version—big and strong and dressed in majestic, flowing robes and just sitting there *not looking very happy!* The second impression was God (same look) standing over me with his hand drawn back, ready to strike . . . *still not looking very happy!*

Some of you can probably relate to these mental pictures, can't you? But is this the God of the Bible? Is this the God who wants a loving relationship with us as his children?

And what pictures do we have of Jesus? Are they just as distant and condemning? Wouldn't it be something if Jesus were a person like us? Wouldn't it be something if he walked where we walked? Wouldn't it be something if he could actually be a *friend?*

The amazing news is that he did become a person, he did walk on this earth, and he actually calls us friends. These words to his disciples are for us too: "You are my friends if you do what I command. I no longer call you servants, because a servant does not know his master's business. Instead, I have called you *friends*" (John 15:14–15).

If your head is filled with visions of an aloof, unconcerned Christ, look again. He offers himself to you as friend. Accept his hand. Wouldn't that be something?

PERSONAL REFLECTIONS

1. What distant, harsh images do you have of God or Jesus? Where did these images come from?

2. What are some of the blessings of a good friendship?

3. How can your friendship with Jesus be mutual? What contributions can you make to the relationship?

life response

Spend some time today in prayer or in the Word getting to know your friend Jesus—not asking him for anything except to know him better.

FIFTEEN

Wait
a
Little
Longer

FIELD OF SOULS

Wait a Little Longer

I know these feelings are new to you
I know the mystery and the desire
Have you decided what you're gonna do
When temptation builds a fire?
The heat of passion for a moment
Could burn you for a lifetime to come
One minute's pleasure might put off your pain
But it takes the innocence from the young

(Chorus)
Why don't you wait a little longer
Be a little stronger
Love is patient and I know you're gonna find
If you'll wait a little longer and be a little stronger
You will cherish the love God gives you all in good time

Your world is filled with fewer do's than don'ts
More blacks and whites than grays
To learn the difference between need and want
Will prove you wise beyond your days
It's always easier to do what's wrong
Than to hold out and do what's right
Who said the easy way was always best?
You gotta hold on with all your might
It will be worth the fight for you to . . .

(Repeat Chorus)

We held out for each other before we ever
met, and we held out from each other
until the day we were husband and wife.

Do you not know that your body
is a temple of the Holy Spirit,
who is in you, whom you have received from God?
You are not your own; you were bought at a price.
Therefore honor God with your body.

1 Corinthians 6:19–20

๛

Yes, it's true—there are some matters of Scripture that could be called *gray.* I suppose that some of the debates will never be settled. But there are many, many places where the Word is black and white—clear and to the point. Sexual purity is one such area.

> God wants you to be holy and stay away from sexual sins. He wants each of you to learn to control your own body in a way that is holy and honorable. Don't use your body for sexual sin like people who do not know God. Also, do not wrong or cheat another Christian in this way. The Lord will punish people

who do those things as we have already told you and warned you. *God called us to be holy and does not want us to live in sin.*

(1 Thess. 4:3–7 NCV)

Is that clear enough? Several other passages also speak clearly to sexual issues. But I don't see these teachings as God's way of trying to put a stop to all our fun; rather I see them as reflections of a loving Father trying to protect his children from harm. I think it gladdens the heart of God to see his children enjoying the life he gave us—but only in accordance with his principles and guidelines. His precepts are always for our good.

I met my wife in my first class in the fall semester of my freshman year of college. I was struck by her sweet spirit and by her beautiful smile, which came from deep inside. We married just fourteen months later. Some thought we were too young, and without a doubt, we were naive, but we were in *love*—and hey, the radio said that's all we needed. Why would the Beatles lie?

One of the most precious things Lynn and I carried to our wedding day was our purity. While we weren't perfect in this area, we held out *for* each other before we ever met, and we held out *from* each other until the day we were husband and wife. I thank God that by his grace I was able to hold fast to the good lessons my mom and dad had taught me.

Now I am a father with boys of my own, and I am very aware of the struggles they face. My prayer for my boys is one you can pray if you have children. I pray that God will place people in their paths who will help them walk in holiness. I pray for friends who will encourage purity and discourage anything that will drag their minds down to the lowly and crude elements of thought. I pray that their consciences will be tender and that they will be sensitive to God's plans for their lives beyond the immediate boy-girl relationship. I pray that God will protect them from temptations that might overpower them.

But our children are not the only ones who need to be concerned with holiness. If you and I are honest, we know that we are all just one bad decision away from trouble. We need to be continually on guard against the Evil One who would love to snatch our purity from us even now. And as redeemed followers of Christ, we can encourage everyone around us toward purity and holiness—not holding our noses up in the air as if sexual sin is beneath us, but living in gratitude for God's safekeeping, we can be humble lights shining brightly in a dark universe.

Oh . . . and one more thing. If you have memories of past mistakes that haunt you every time your head hits the pillow—memories of something you did years, weeks, or days ago—I would remind you of one of the sweetest promises ever given: "If we confess our sins, he is faithful and just, and will forgive our sins and cleanse us from *all* unrighteousness" (1 John 1:9 RSV).

Guilt is a terrible motivator. Guilt only reminds us of failure and, for many, brings despair and zaps us of the strength to resist temptation. The enemy craftily uses guilt to keep us from our pursuit of godliness and holiness. He knows that if we accept God's forgiveness, we will be liberated to live joyfully before our Father.

Allow the Lord to bring forgiveness and light to the dark, secret places of your heart. He will give you a new start.

PERSONAL REFLECTIONS

1. Why do you think God reserves sex for marriage?

2. Have you allowed yourself to rationalize "little sexual indiscretions"?

3. Are you a humble light of purity to those around you or a self-righteous foghorn? What can you do to change your approach?

4. How can guilt keep you from godliness and holiness? Have you allowed guilt to discourage you in your efforts to be like Christ?

5. How can you deal with guilt so that it doesn't hinder your growth?

life response

Read the following Scriptures and take to your heart God's clear teaching on sexual purity: Romans 13:13–14; 1 Corinthians 6:9–10, 13–20; Ephesians 5:3–7; Colossians 3:5; 1 Thessalonians 4:3–8.

Growing

*f*rom the album

THE WAY HOME

Growing

(Chorus)
I'm growing; I don't like it
I'm growing and it hurts
I love you but I'm tired
Guess I've got a lot to learn
Yeah, guess I've got a lot to learn

Don't leave me here
You said you would not forsake me
But you never said that you wouldn't break me
To make me over in the image of you
In the dark night of the soul
When there's no comfort in prayin'
Not a moment's pleasure in strayin'
You're the only shelter I know

(Repeat Chorus)

When feelings fail
When "close enough" isn't good enough
When "full enough" just isn't full enough
Your grace will be sufficient for me
No wind to sail
No rain to water the flower
In my most desperate hour
You will be the strength that I need

(Repeat Chorus)

While change and
growth are difficult,
the blessings of growth far
exceed the discomforts of change.

So neither he who plants nor he who waters is anything,
but only God, who makes things grow.

1 Corinthians 3:7

⌣

A young friend recently went to one of my con-
certs with her dad and heard my song "Growing." Being a
part of a wonderful Christian home and godly parents, she
asked her father, "Daddy, is he saying that he doesn't *want* to
grow to be more like Jesus?" May God bless her and prolong
her sweet innocence.

Certainly I want to continue to be conformed to the image
of my Savior. This desire should be the highest priority in the
life of every believer. It's just that it's easier to say you want to
grow when you're not in the *process* of growth. Growth means
being nudged toward change; it means being stretched
beyond our comfort zones. Growth is sometimes painful, and
I'm not particularly fond of pain.

My friend reminded his little girl of the discomfort of their recent move. They had moved to a new town, but it was unfamiliar; into a nice neighborhood, but it was filled with strangers; and into a new house, but it wasn't like their old one. To a child, these are *the* issues of life. "Where are my friends? Where is my stuff? Which box did you say it was in?" This appropriate and timely reminder of a personal portrait of change proved to be a good lesson for this little girl. It's a good lesson for all of us.

Have you ever experienced a dark period in your walk with the Lord? If you haven't, maybe you'd better prepare. Some of these dark nights require a whole new level of faith, and if you cooperate, they will take you to another new level of faith. Dark nights require a faith not based on feelings. They demand prayer when you may not feel like praying. They lead you to solitude with God when you'd rather have people around. And they plunge you into the depths of Scripture, even when you don't feel like hearing its truths.

Growing also demands that you take personal inventory. This means assessing the current value of the things that have accumulated in your life—I'm talking physical, mental, and spiritual assessment. And once you have taken inventory, the next step is *cleaning*.

My wife and I are different kinds of cleaners. (Now, I hope and pray that what I'm about to tell you is not some psychological indicator of my spiritual health. Yikes! Well, here goes.) Lynn is thorough. I mean, she gets down to the dirt and works from the bottom up. You might not see any improvement for a while, but when the chore is done, you

have something *clean.* I, on the other hand, am more of a surface cleaner. I want it to look good on the outside, and I want
quick results. Sometimes this means cleaning the surface and
postponing the hard stuff for later.

I think the more spiritually correct cleaning method would
have to be the get-down-to-the-gritty version. This is the kind
required for personal, internal housecleaning. When tackling
our inner houses, we can't be primarily concerned with the
outside appearance. The outside will usually take care of itself
and will reflect what's inside.

I guess there's nothing wrong with stuffing things in a
closet or a drawer until you have time to deal with them, but
the danger is that when things are out of sight, they're often,
indeed, out of mind. If you're going to tuck something away
to be dealt with later, just be sure you *do* deal with it. The
longer you ignore the junk in the drawer or closet of your life,
the more likely that the following things will happen:

- You'll be tempted to add even more junk to the pile.

- You'll continue to put off a chore you already put off
  once.

- You'll be haunted by the knowledge that you will
  have to deal with it *someday.*

- Some of the stuff you're hiding will eventually begin
  to *smell!*

Sometimes we have the luxury of choosing to take a personal inventory, like when we go to a spiritual seminar or
retreat; at other times, periods of inventory and reflection are

forced upon us. Either way, God is faithful and good, and he will not require more from us than we can handle. While change and growth are difficult, the blessings of growth far exceed the discomforts of change.

You don't have to clean out all the junk in your life in one day, but you do have to start somewhere. Take a long, hard look into your life and heart, zero in on just one or two things that need to change, and then trust the God who knows you much better than you know yourself and allow him to guide you to new levels of faith.

PERSONAL REFLECTIONS

1. What passages of growth has God already led you through? What was the outcome?

2. What pain have you experienced in growth? Looking back, can you now say it was worth it?

3. What kind of cleaner are you when it comes to spiritual matters?

4. What one area can you ask God today to help you grow in?

life response

Consider a current difficulty or stress you are experiencing. Look at it in light of how God can use it to help you grow. Commit to cooperating with him in the growth process.

SEVENTEEN

Field of Souls

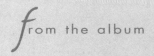

*f*rom the album

FIELD OF SOULS

Field of Souls

(Chorus)
We work the field of souls
Together you and I
Some fields are blooming now
Other fields are dry
We are not the same
But differences aside
We will work the field of souls
Together you and I

One is off to foreign soil
To work a distant land
Another anchors close to home
To hold a neighbor's hand
Who has served the Father most
And who has labored best?

That life devoted to our God
That devotion will be blessed

(Repeat Chorus)

One shouts the gospel in the streets
For everyone to hear
He's bold to everyone he meets
The Word is loud and clear
Another cries alone and prays
In silence on her knees
Before the throne day after day
Where human eyes don't see

(Repeat Chorus)

FIELD OF SOULS by Wayne Watson
© 1995 Word Music (A Div. of WORD MUSIC) and Material Music (Admin. by WORD MUSIC).
All Rights Reserved. Used By Permission.

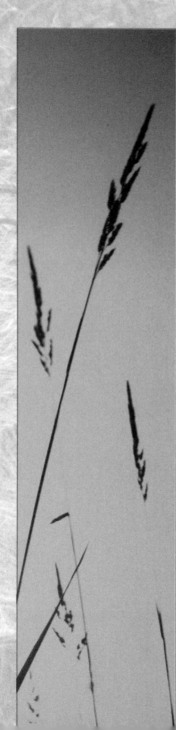

To doubt
our worth
is to doubt
our Creator.

God has arranged the parts in the body,
every one of them, just as he wanted them to be.
If they were all one part, where would the body be?
As it is, there are many parts, but one body.
1 Corinthians 12:18–20

᠅

*G*od is the host of a universal variety show, and you are in it. In fact, every eye that reads these words is a window into the soul of a star in his show. Although all the participants have much in common, each star is uniquely talented to serve God's special purpose.

When you ask children "What do you want to be when you grow up?" you get all kinds of answers. You find aspiring ballplayers, ballerinas, doctors, firemen, carpenters, truck drivers, school teachers, and everything in between. Where do these varied aspirations come from? I believe they come from a divinely implanted urge to please our heavenly Father and to maximize the gifts he has given us.

When I was a boy, I wanted to be a baseball player when I grew up. I remember thinking, *Wow, if I could play professional ball, what a great witness I could be!* Oh well, it wasn't meant to be. But I do have friends who play pro sports, and I'll let you in on some great news: Lots of them love the Lord more than the sports they play. They believe they are on a mission from God to be his ambassadors in the locker rooms and on the playing fields.

They will bump shoulders with people whom most of us will never meet; and as they go about exercising the gifts and talents God has given them, they will shine the light of Christ into some very dark places. Thank God that he gave these men and women the talent that would place them in the paths of the needy.

Some of us may have difficulty being thankful for the opportunities of others because we wish so badly that *we* could have the same opportunities. We compare ourselves with others and wish we were different than we are. Have you ever heard a powerful speaker who could move an audience to tears and to a greater commitment to God and wished that *you* had such a gift? Or have you ever sat entranced, listening to a voice that sweetly softened hearts with song, and longed to be used by God in such a way yourself? Perhaps you left the gathering thinking, *That's what I should be doing. God would really be proud of me if I could do that!*

I think our dissatisfaction with who we are hurts God's heart. After all, he is the one who made us. You've heard the saying, "God doesn't make junk!" And it's true: To doubt our worth is to doubt our Creator.

Some of our self-doubt is caused by the notion that all Christians should be the same. May I point out that the Bible *doesn't* say, "Be conformed to one another." Rather, God's Word says that we are "predestined to be conformed to the likeness of his Son" (Rom. 8:29). Some church bodies—with the best of intentions—imply that anyone who really loves Jesus will "walk this way, talk this way, dress this way, cut his hair this way, read this, and not listen to that." Sometimes these good intentions can get out of hand.

Obviously there are some hard-and-fast theological guidelines. There is not really much debate on, say, sexual purity. God's Word is pretty clear on that, isn't it? But we have to be careful not to add our own prejudices and personal tastes to God's divine Word. To shave off the unique edges that God has built into each of us would not only be a shame, it would be an insult to the Creator. "Oh, Lord, I know you built us this way, but now we are going to perfect each other by forming each other into our own images." We have to be careful that any "perfecting" we do is by God's leading and by his inspiration.

God has placed us all in the field of souls—each one bringing special talents; each one playing a part. Some of you are tender, soft-hearted, kind, and gentle by nature. Others have the textbook "Type A" personality that runs in high gear at all times. To deny that God created us with different temperaments is foolish. To insist that we can only coexist in peace by having the same disposition limits God's fantastic variety show.

Fulfill the potential God has planted in you; develop the gifts he has given you. You moms who wait at home until the kids get off the bus, open your arms knowing that you are fulfilling a need in the kingdom. You who work in schools, serving lunch or teaching children, know you are performing a vital function—you are nurturing young minds and hearts for eternity. You office workers, construction workers, CEOs, secretaries, truck drivers, computer technicians—whoever you are and whatever you do, be and do it with all your might as unto the Lord (Col. 3:23).

When you love the Lord with all your heart, wherever you are is a mission field. You and I can work the field at lunch or on the job. There are people everywhere in need of the light of Christ, and the Lord needs all of us to do the work. The job cannot, will not, get done if we are all doing the same tasks. Make God look good (bring glory to him) as you do your part in his amazing variety show. God will use you to touch your world as I touch mine.

PERSONAL REFLECTIONS

1. What special talents has God given you? How are you using them?

2. Do you sometimes compare yourself to someone who has different talents? What talents has God given you different from what he's given that person?

3. How can doubting our worth be the same as doubting our Creator?

4. What is the difference between *unity* and *uniformity*? How can diverse people be united in purpose even if they are not uniform in gifts and perspectives?

life response

Thank God for a specific gift he has given you and look for opportunities to use it to work the field of souls.

EIGHTEEN

Perception

The Way Home

Perception

They saw me eatin'
At the table with the sinners
Tax collectors
The harlots and the thieves
Sometimes I wonder
Should I be more careful
'Bout what people are thinking
What they choose to believe?

They saw me talking
To that woman at the fountain
I heard 'em whisper,
"What's he doing with her?"
Guess I can suffer
In people's estimation
For the transformation
Of one sinner to occur

(Chorus)
Not losin' sleep over some bad perception
What people believe to be true
I'm gonna risk my reputation for the harvest
The fields are ready
There's a lot to do

They'll see me crucified
Hanging on a mountain
They'll say, "I guess
He's just a criminal too"
I hope they're listening
To hear me when I whisper
"Father, forgive them
They don't know what they do"

(Repeat Chorus)

The fields are ready
There's a lot to do
The fields are ready
There's a lot to do
The fields are ready

(Repeat Chorus)

PERCEPTIONS by Wayne Watson
© 1997 Word Music (A Div. of WORD MUSIC) and Material Music (Admin. by WORD MUSIC).
All Rights Reserved. Used By Permission.

149

God help us to be
willing to risk
our reputation
to see one lonely
soul come to the
truth of Christ.

Stop judging by mere appearances,
and make a right judgment.

John 7:24

ॐ

"Perception is everything," he said. I'd heard that statement before, but this time, it really hit a nerve.

Now don't get me wrong; perceptions can be important. After all, the Bible tells us to avoid even the "appearance of evil" (1 Thess. 5:22). So perceptions are certainly not *nothing,* but they aren't everything either. Too often, perceptions lead to hasty conclusions that are just plain wrong.

If Christ had been concerned with his reputation and his social standing within the community and among the religious elite, he would have been frozen in his attempts to reach the world. But our Lord was more concerned with the needs of the hurting than the approval of the establishment. Our

CHAPTER EIGHTEEN

Savior was a man of righteous character and absolute obedience to his Father.

Can't you imagine the rumors that must have circulated regarding the company he kept. He ate with sinners; he conversed with hated tax collectors; why, he even talked to a Samaritan woman whose "loose" lifestyle was known to all. "Why is he talking to her?" the gossip would begin. "Do they *know* each other?" someone else would ask, with all the illicit implications. And then the snickers would accompany the inappropriate and inaccurate conclusions.

Or imagine a group of teenage boys walking past the hill where three Roman crosses stood. "They got another one. He must have done some heavy-duty crime," one of them says. "Yeah, why else would they crucify him? King of the Jews? Yeah, right."

When perception is everything, people are guilty by association. You know, "Where there's smoke, there's fire." Right?

Wrong. Because Jesus did not allow perceptions to stifle his work, the Light of the World sat down with sinners and lovingly *shined* on them, offering forgiveness and redemption. Because he could see the pain in men's souls, he gently called tax collectors to eat at his table. Because Jesus loved hurting individuals more than a glowing reputation, he spoke kindly with a woman who was deeply ashamed and embarrassed at her five failed marriages and her current illicit relationship. His words may have been the only encouraging words she had heard all week. Was her life ever the same after her brief dialogue with the Son of God?

Imagine yourself in this position: A dear friend has a terrible and destructive drinking problem. You know his favorite after-work watering hole, and after prayerful consideration (important!), you decide to surprise him at the entrance of that particular establishment. Your motives are pure, and your action demonstrates a Christ-like love and concern for your friend. The damage to himself and his family have gone far enough, and your prayer is that this awkward, humiliating, loving confrontation will shake him from his destructive routine. But if your pastor or that pillar-of-the-church elder drives by and sees you at the entrance to the bar, their perception could lead them to believe something that is completely false. And if some holier-than-thou gossip should see you, you're sunk! What will you do?

Let's pray that we would all aspire to live in high and noble character, motivated by love for God and souls in need. God help us to be willing to risk our name or stellar reputation to see one lonely soul come to a knowledge of the truth of Christ. Live as Christ did—more considerate of the needs of the wounded than the perceptions of the religious.

PERSONAL REFLECTIONS

1. Have you ever been the victim of judgement based on inaccurate perceptions? How did you feel?

2. Has your inaccurate perception of a brother or sister in Christ ever led to wrong judgment? How can you prevent this from happening again?

3. Is it ever important to consider how our behavior looks to others? Why? Whose reputation is at stake besides our own?

4. What guidelines can help you discern when to do or say something even if it makes you look bad?

life response

Determine today to be a man or woman of integrity, to put the needs of others above your concern for status.

NINETEEN

Come
Home

Come Home

I looked out across the field
At the sundown gold
Don't feel so young anymore
But sure don't feel old
And I remember you as a child
Running 'round free
You would play through the day into nighttime
Till you could not see

(Chorus)
Come home—come home
Night is falling but the lights are on
Come home—come home
Night is falling and it won't be long
I'll turn my head
And you'll be grown

I stood in the dark by the window
Lookin' for your lights
I sleep better knowing everybody's home
And everybody's all right
Just one of those things that happens
When you care so much
And you pray to keep from worryin'
Then you worry you ain't prayin' enough

(Repeat Chorus)

We are all just children
Even your mama and me
And everybody gone before us
From this family
And God, the good, good Father watches
Those he calls his own
And one day when we're through growin'
He's gonna call us home and he'll say

Come home—come home
Night has fallen but the lights are on
Come home—come home
Night has fallen and it's been so long
Since we've all been together
Gonna be here forever
Come home, come on home

In every house,
I have found a
windowpane
from which I
can watch the
comings and
goings of my
precious children.

The Lord will watch over your coming and going
both now and forevermore.

Psalm 121:8

ॐ

*E*very parent has more than a few monumental
moments on file that define him or her as Dad or Mom.
Mom's premier moment is often her starring role in the birth
of her babies. That moment defines a role that occupies most
of her life and energy. While us dads are obviously separated
from the physical trials of bringing a new life into the world,
only a few seconds pass before we assume the role of guardian,
protector, and provider.

My family and I have lived in several different houses over
the years. In each one, I have found a special spot—a strategic
post, a lookout. This vantage point has become a definitive
position for me, and the moments I have spent there partially

define who I am. In every house, I have found a windowpane (also spelled *pain*) from which I can watch the comings and goings of my precious children.

When my boys were in preschool, I watched them playing in the sandbox with the neighbor kids. I remember secretly wishing for some minor altercation that would require my presence and wisdom. Dad to the rescue! Even then, it occurred to me that I wouldn't always be around to step in. "God," I prayed, "you'll have to teach me how to release these children into your hands."

As time passed, I stood at another window, diligently manning my post, peering through the dark for familiar headlights. As car after car passed by—none the one I waited for—my heart rate increased. I would think of the multitude of things that could go wrong for a competent, but inexperienced, young driver. When the Apostle Paul wrote, "Do not be anxious about anything" (Phil. 4:6), did he know about vague four-way stops, caution lights, and speed limits?

But I've begun to realize that there aren't enough windows in the world to allow me a clear view of every potential hurt my kids will face or every obstacle they'll encounter. You'd think a lifetime of church attendance and a limited, but solid, awareness of Scripture would quiet some of these tremors, but only a minute-by-minute faith in God can keep my window panes from fogging over with worry and anxiety.

Are you conscious throughout your day that your heavenly Father is watching over you? I wonder if God is more at rest when everyone is "home" and under his protection? Does it grieve the heart of God when we stray from the view of his window of right fellowship? I believe we can bring pleasure to our Father by remaining in his view, even with all our busy comings and goings. One defining picture of our loving Father is of him standing at the window pane of heaven, ever watchful, always ready to protect and defend, with a heart overflowing with love and affection.

Stay close to the throne.

PERSONAL REFLECTIONS

1. What special moments or activities define you as a parent or define your mom or dad as parent?

2. What parental characteristics do you see in our heavenly Father?

3. As loving parent, what does God do to protect us from harm?

4. As loving parent, does God protect us from all harm? Why or why not?

5. What can you do to insure that you stay close to God's throne?

life response

Take a moment to consider whether you are standing in view of heaven's window pane. If the cares and "treasures" of this life have pulled you from his view, go to your Father in prayer and ask him to help you reposition your heart.

TWENTY

A Beautiful Place

A Beautiful Place

If I had my way, I must admit
If I called every play of the game
I'd pray for good times
Blue sky and sunshine
And avoid with a passion the pain

But with every blow from an angry wind
And with every dark shadow that falls
There's a better view up around the bend
Where this puzzle makes some sense after all

(Chorus)
Mistakes and misfortunes will come and go
But to try and to fail is no disgrace
Sometimes a rough and a rocky road
Can take you to a beautiful place

Is there anyone looking back in faith
That can deny that the Father knows best?
But at the time and place for the life of you
You saw no reason, no good for the test

But now remembering as you've watched his hand
Put the color to your black and white dreams
Maybe one more time past what you can see
The trouble of the moment's not as bad as it seems

(Repeat Chorus)

And the unspoiled beauty of the wisdom of God
Lies in the wilderness
Up there beyond the easy reach
Where the journey takes a little more faith, I guess

(Repeat Chorus)

Don't let fear of the unknown or anxiety over the future keep you from taking your first steps of faith today.

In the way of righteousness there is life;
along that path is immortality.
Proverbs 12:28

☙

*T*ry explaining the beauty of the northern Rockies viewed from a height of 30,000 feet to someone who's intensely afraid of flying, and you'll probably be met with something less than enthusiasm. "Uh huh . . . I'm sure it's a wonderful sight." It wouldn't matter whether this person soared above Mount Everest or the wastelands of some desert country, the fear of flying would outweigh any desire to see the world from a bird's eye view.

If you could whisper into the tiny ear of an almost full-term but as yet unborn child, you might say, "Hey, there's a wonderful world out here! There are people who can't wait to hug and kiss you and shower you with all kinds of love and affection. You'll find delicious food (mashed peas and strained carrots?), warm sunshine, and beautiful snow. There's a whole world of experience just waiting for you!" But most little darlings would probably reply, "No thanks, pal. I'm warm and cozy right where I am. In here, *I'm the man!*" (Or *woman,* as the case may be.)

Most of us have some degree of fear of the unknown. Some adventures are simply too mysterious to get excited about. The promise of *adventure* isn't always worth the effort or the anxiety.

My sons once asked me to join them on a hike in the Rocky Mountains. At the end of this particular series of trails, they told me, was a spectacular, "must see" view. But I must admit, my vision of the obstacles before me was much more powerful than the promise of a beautiful view. All I could see was a difficult journey and a trail filled with rocks, holes, low-lying limbs, and vicious varmints! But eventually, the promise of spending a few private hours with my two sons overcame my fear. And as you might expect, the view at the end of the path was well worth the difficulty of the journey. For my trouble, I was rewarded with a breathtaking picture of nature in its unspoiled, undisturbed state—a perspective I could never have imagined from my comfort zone below.

The next time you feel overwhelmed by the journey, remember that you are not "there" yet. When your day is full of disappointment, when you're wounded, or when your progress is slowed by obstacles along the way, remember God's promises and his faithfulness. While we can't see with his eyes, we know we can trust his heart. Don't let fear of the unknown or anxiety over the future keep you from taking your first steps of faith today. Those steps just might take you to a beautiful place.

PERSONAL REFLECTIONS

1. What fears do you have that keep you from stepping out in faith into new spiritual adventures?

2. What comforts are you hesitant to give up in exchange for spritual growth?

3. Recall a particular experience where you finally ventured out in faith, even though you were afraid, and the outcome was positive. What lessons did you learn from that experience?

4. Recall an experience where you chose the path of faith only to find increased difficulty. What valuable lessons did you learn on that path?

5. How have you grown in your trust in God through your life's journey?

life response

Evaluate the difficulties in your current path of faith. Ask God to give you the grace to see the difficulties in your path as stepping stones to a beautiful place.

TWENTY-ONE

More of You

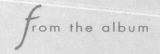

*f*rom the album

A BEAUTIFUL PLACE

More of You

Thought I could give her everything
The fairy tale—the rainbow's end
But happiness is not for sale
The rules of God, I could not bend
Foolish and young, you set your eyes
On the American dream
Then when you faint from the run
You realize the answer is easy to see

(Chorus)
All she really needs from me is more of you
That's all she really needs from me
I know it is; I know it's true
More understanding, more tenderness
A love that goes beyond my humanness
That's all she really needs from me
Is more of you—more of you—more of you

Now today, I'm not the same
As the man I used to be
But the very best that can be said
Jesus is alive and well in me
But every now and then
The pressure builds—anxiety grows
Old habits reappear—frustration's real
But inside I know, I know

(Repeat Chorus)

(Bridge)
So this will be my prayer today
The same one tomorrow, forever
That I will keep your love displayed
For all around to see
That's all she really needs from me

What Lynn needs is more of him in me
—more of his tenderness, more of his
patience, more of his love.

We, who with unveiled faces
all reflect the Lord's glory,
are being transformed into his likeness
with ever-increasing glory.

2 Corinthians 3:18

॰

hen Mama ain't happy, ain't nobody happy."
While the T-shirt slogan is intended to be a joke, it reminds
me of the old saying, "Many a truth is said in jest." When one
person in a family is unhappy, a cloud seems to spread over
the entire bunch, doesn't it?

Part of caring for those you love is shouldering their bur-
dens and easing their hurts. Unfortunately, many of the
wounds and hurts inflicted on the ones we love come from
inside the camp—the home.

I don't know about you, but sometimes I find it easier to be
a godly mirror of Christ out "there," in public, than I do in my
own home. Maybe that's because I'm part of a generation that

is more concerned with who people *think* we are than with who we *really* are.

Let's face it, if you're a Christian and if you want others to know you're a Christian, you will be careful to walk in a manner worthy of the name of Christ. If you've been taught the Scriptures, you will try to live them to the glory of God in view of friends and strangers. And that's good! Friends and strangers are watching, so keep it up. But too often, our intense zeal to live and walk in righteousness before others is often checked at the door *of our own homes!* And that's exactly what Satan wants. He loves using our homes as battleground for spiritaul warfare. As James said "Brothers and sisters, this ought not be" (James 3:10).

I love my wife, my girl, Lynn. Even after twenty-four years of marriage (as of this writing), I still think of her constantly when I travel. I love more things about her than I can count. But I tell you, I can speak more harshly to her than I ever do to strangers, I am more impatient with her over insignificant issues than I am with those in the world over "important" things, and I allow anger and moodiness to surface at the drop of a hat—and all with this precious creature whom I dearly love. Again I say, "This ought not be!"

These past few years, I have begun to put more effort into being Christlike in the privacy of my home—where no one sees and no one applauds. I have learned that what Lynn needs from me is not more expensive clothes or exotic vacations; what Lynn needs is more of *God* in me—more of his tenderness, more of his patience, more of his love. I fail at my efforts to be like Jesus more than I like to admit, but by his grace, I will have more of him in me tomorrow than I do today.

Seek God's smile of approval not only when you walk as a light in the darkness of the outside world, but also when you walk into the privacy of your home.

PERSONAL REFLECTIONS

1. Is there an unresolved hurt between you and some-one in your family? If so, what can you do to set things right?

2. What in your relationship with your family most quickly arouses your impatience or anger? What examples from Christ's life teach you how to better respond in those situations?

3. Who, outside your home, do you try to be a reflec-tion of Christ to? What can you learn from your behavior with those people that you can bring into your home?

life response

Examine your treatment of those you love most. Ask God to increase your love and kind-ness toward them; make a conscious effort to cooperate with God as he works in your heart.

TWENTY-TWO

Walk in the Dark

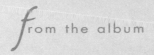
A BEAUTIFUL PLACE

Walk in the Dark

Where are you taking me
Why are we turning here
This road is strange to me
This path is not so clear

Must be the place where my doubt turns to faith
Where I close my eyes and take your hand

(Chorus)
I'd rather walk in the dark with Jesus
Than to walk in the light on my own
I'd rather go through the valley of the shadow with him
Than to dance on the mountains alone
I'd rather follow wherever he leads me
Than to go where none before me have gone
I'd rather walk in the dark with Jesus
Than to walk in the light on my own

I've made some plans you know
Mapped out a strategy
Somebody tell me, where did the seasons go?
Have you forgotten me?

I've heard the darkest hour is just before the dawn
And wherever you are the sun will shine

(Repeat Chorus)

(Bridge)
There will be shadows—but I won't be shaken
'Cause you've never forsaken a vow
You've never failed me before this I know
And, Jesus, you won't fail me now

(Repeat Chorus)

"Faith is walking on the edge of all the light you have and then taking one more step."

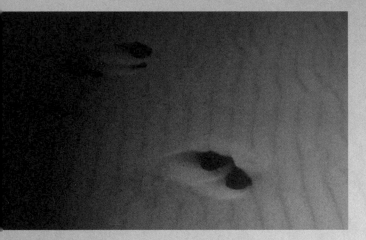

Even the darkness will not be dark to you;
the night will shine like the day,
for darkness is as light to you.

Psalm 139:12

უ

When I first met my wife, she had a poster in her house that said, "Faith is walking on the edge of all the light you have and then taking one more step." I can still see that poster in my mind today.

It takes no faith to walk where we can see. We can all navigate the paths where all the obstacles and hazards are visible, can't we? But when the lights are out, I want to be holding on to someone who knows the way, someone who's walked this path before, someone who can steer me away from danger.

As I grow, I'm less dependent on my own strength, my own grip. I know the phrase may be somewhat overused, but honestly, I'm learning more and more to *hold to the hand of*

Jesus. I don't trust my own grip as much as I used to. These days, I'm more inclined to trust that God's hand is strong enough to hold me—even when I have no strength to hold to him.

When "Walk in the Dark" first came out, I received a few letters reminding me that the Bible says, "We walk in the light, as he is in the light" and "Jesus is the light of the world." I believe those words with all my heart. This song is not about spiritual darkness—when I met Christ, spiritual darkness disappeared. This song is about the times when the lights are out in my life, when the future is cloudy and dark and I can't see.

I have to admit that there have been times when I've felt my prayers were not only *unanswered,* but *not even heard.* Feeling ignored by the heavenly Father is a desperate place for someone who claims to put trust in him. That's the kind of darkness I'm talking about. Have you been there? Have you walked to the edge of all the light you had and feared taking that next step because you weren't sure his hand would reach out to catch you? I think we all know how that feels.

There was a movie where the hero, Indiana Jones, was required to step out in faith over a great cavern—a deep pit of nothingness. When he took a step, instead of falling into the depths, a pathway materialized under his feet. "But that's fantasy, a movie!" I hear you say. But that is exactly what God does for us. When we step out in faith, he provides the way. He shines a light on our dark path. In fact, he transforms darkness into light. Listen to what David says in Psalm 18: "You, O Lord, keep my lamp burning; my God turns my darkness into light" (v. 28).

I have to believe that God keeps all his promises. Our lives are not limited to what we see before us today—our lives are a walk, a journey. And although we cannot see all the way down the path, God can. By faith I say,

> There will be shadows—but I won't be shaken,
> 'Cause you've never forsaken one vow.
> You've never failed me before this I know,
> And, Jesus, you won't fail me now.

PERSONAL REFLECTIONS

1. Recall a time when your life seemed dark. How did you get through it?

2. How can you use the memory of God's presence in past difficulties to help you through present and future ones?

3. What's the difference between spiritual darkness and dark circumstances? Can Chrisians experience dark circumstances while still being in the light? If so, how?

4. What benefits have you gained from past valleys of darkness? How has your faith grown through past

life response

Try praising God the next time you find yourself in dark circumstances. Praise him for how he's guided you in the past; praise him for his faithfulness; praise him for his unconditional, never-ending love. Praise and fear cannot reside together in your heart.

TWENTY-THREE

That's Not Jesus

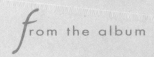

That's Not Jesus

I read the mornin' paper
To my surprise and shame
Said a black eye of embarrassment
Been attached to Jesus' name
Some mortal man convicted
Of some moldy moral sin
And the skeptics wag their tongues and say
"There goes that Jesus again"

The story graced the TV
And the magazines too long
And if my heart ain't broken yet
There must be somethin' wrong
Because but for the grace of God
I know it could be me
And all that's left for me to do
Is to help the world to see

(Chorus)
That's not Jesus
He doesn't carry on that way
Just some flesh and blood like you and me
Somehow gone astray
That's not Jesus, no
No matter what "they" say
He doesn't need me to defend him
He just wants me to obey
He just wants me to obey

Have you seen the masterpiece
Of Jesus on the Cross?
Well, if he's still a-hangin' there
I'm hopeless— I am lost
I believe the tomb is empty
And the stone's been rolled away
And because of all this trouble
I still feel compelled to say

(Repeat Chorus)

(Bridge)
And if your vision of him
Has gotten somehow blurred
By some stumbling soldier in the field
I'd like to say, "I'm sorry"
And remind you of one thing
One day all the truth will be revealed

(Repeat Chorus)

some folks' only
perception of Jesus
comes through what
they see in religion.

*Let your light shine before men, that they may see your good
deeds and praise your Father in heaven.*

Matthew 5:16

᠉

Over the centuries, Jesus has been appropriated to all
kinds of pigeon holes and has been seen from various
perspectives—many of them wrong, or at least incomplete.

Some folks' only perception of Jesus comes through what
they see in religion. Given the multitude of denominations
and churches, quite divergent pictures are conveyed. If a wan-
dering soul stumbles into a formal, liturgical church, his
impression of Christ might be quite serious and reverential. A
spectacular cathedral evokes a sense of awe. The power of traditional hymns represents a standard that isn't swayed by contemporary thought or pattern. To some, these impressions

might testify that, indeed, God is the same today, yesterday, and forever.

If the same person steps into a contemporary praise service, with loud, joyful songs played by a worship band, they might get a totally different picture of Jesus. Personal testimonies given in everyday vernacular are witness to Christ's relevancy and impact on today's society.

Neither the serious, reverential view nor the contemporary, relevant view are improper. Both are partial pictures of who Jesus is. But some pictures of Jesus are completely distorted and make me want to stand up and shout, "That's not Jesus!" Many of you may recall the ruckus a few years back when some visable religious personalities were exposed as living less than exemplary lives. Everytime I heard reports of the scandals, something inside of me cringed and ached at the same time. I wanted to shout to the world, "That's not the Jesus I know!" I felt embarrassed that the name of Christ, which I hold so dear, was being associated with people caught in shameful moral failure. The cause of Christ sufferered! Relationships nurtured so that lost friends would be drawn to the Christ in us were suddenly knocked off course.

Whenever an insult is hurled at my faith, my first response is often a defensive one. But I'm learning that the eternal truth of the living God has managed to survive a history of attacks without my feeble attempts to defend it; our call is to *obey* and to *shine* as lights in the world. God will vindicate himself.

I'm still irritated and sometimes offended at the way some present the truth of Christ. We must all take care that our representation of him is clothed in a humble heart, compassion for the lost, and understanding for the wounded. Our stance is not to be one of arrogance or vain displays that point the world to us and our talents rather than to Christ. While God is faithful to empower us to do his bidding, sometimes it is difficult for us humans to distinguish between supernatural enabling and self-glorifying exhibition.

As Christ's representative here on earth, allow the Holy Spirit to direct you day by day and second by precious second into a walk that pleases and glorifies the Master, so that when people see you they will say, "Hey, that person looks like Jesus."

PERSONAL REFLECTIONS

1. Where have your perceptions of Jesus come from? How have they changed over the years?

2. When people look at your life, what perception of Jesus do they get?

3. Have you ever reacted in an un-Christlike manner in an effort to defend your faith in Christ? What is wrong with that picture? How might you respond differently?

4. In living your life to point others to Jesus, do you ever confuse "supernatural enabling and self-glorifying exhibition"? What steps can you take to grow in your ability to discern the two?

life response

Live your life as if you are the only picture of Jesus some people will ever see.

TWENTY-FOUR

Home Free

Home Free

I'm trying hard not to think you unkind
But heavenly Father
If you know my heart
Surely you can read my mind
Good people underneath a sea of grief
Some get up and walk away
Some will find ultimate relief

(Chorus)
Home free—eventually
At the ultimate healing
We will be home free
Home free
Oh, I've got a feeling
At the ultimate healing
We will be home free

196

Out in the corridors we pray for life
A mother for her baby
A husband for his wife
Sometimes the good die young
It's sad but true
And while we pray for one more heartbeat
The real comfort is with you

Pain has little mercy
Suffering's no respecter of age
Of race or position
I know every prayer gets answered
But the hardest one to pray is slow to come,
"Oh Lord, not mine
But your will be done"

(Repeat Chorus)

The death of
someone you love
can generate a
long list of
questions.

In keeping with his promise
we are looking forward to a new heaven and a new earth,
the home of righteousness.

2 Peter 3:13

uch has been written about why bad things happen to good people. It makes for good reading and insight, until some of the bad things start happening to *you.* Then all the great books and advice go in one ear and out the other, and the never-ending *why* begins.

The death of someone you love can generate a long list of questions. As quickly as one question fades, another takes its place.

Sometimes I just want to know what's going on, but it's up to the Lord to discern whether or not to tell me. Most of the time, I suppose, I'm in a "need-to-know" relationship with the

Father; and sometimes, apparently, he thinks I just don't need to know!

When a loved family member or friend is taken from us, it's never in accordance with *our* plans or *our* timing. If death comes suddenly, we regret not being able to say what we wanted and needed to say; if death comes slowly and our loved one lingers in pain, we ask why God allows such suffering.

If we picture God as an unfeeling, cosmic bully rather than a loving Father, it's easy to allow such questions to drive us from his presence. We may fear that God will strike us down if doubt dares to surface in our minds. But I don't think God is surprised or angered by our questions. God knows what we are made of. The psalmist wrote in the 103rd, "The Lord has mercy on those who respect him as a father has mercy on his children. He knows how we were made; he remembers that we are dust" (vv. 13–14 NCV).

A good father doesn't recoil in horror in the presence of an inquisitive child, does he? If he did, the child would respond in discouragement and defeat, "Oh, I *knew* you wouldn't understand! I'll never bring *this* up again!" Rather, a good father meets questions with patience and understanding; he offers peace and comfort when life doesn't make sense.

If an earthly father can handle doubts and questions from a child, God can certainly be trusted to be patient and help us with our doubts as well—surely he isn't intimidated by our questions. If God really longs for our fellowship, and I believe he does, isn't it possible that inquisitive dialogue from his children is precious to him? A loving father values and holds in high regard *any* time spent in intimate fellowship and meaningful communication with his child.

But we must be careful that our questions don't turn insolent or spiteful. We mustn't forget, we are dealing with the *Almighty God*—he is the one who has mercifully granted us an audience. Still, when we are haunted by questions of *why,* we can come boldly before the throne of grace—trusting that God will see us through—or perhaps simply give us grace to trust him with things we cannot understand.

My father died in the spring of 1997. During his last days, I actually envied his destination. I imagined his future audience with the Savior and all the saints and his reunion with his mother, father, brothers, and sister. I smiled inside as I realized that he no longer had to worry about the farm, the bank, or the stock market. His focus was being directed to more important things.

My dad is home. So are many of those you love. During times of loss I have sometimes thought, *Dear Lord, I sure do hope that what I've believed all these years is true.* And it always comes back to settle in my heart that through Christ God has taken away the sting of death and has prepared a better place for us—a place we call home.

CHAPTER TWENTY-FOUR

PERSONAL REFLECTIONS

1. What questions have you asked in the wake of death or hardship?

2. Have you ever doubted God's love? When? How did you become reassured of his love?

3. How do you think God feels about your questions and doubts?

4. Think about this statement: "God is 'big' enough to handle our questions without being intimidated." How can this understanding change how you handle your doubts?

life response

Begin today being honest with God about your emotions, your fears, and your doubts. Spend some time reading the following passages from Psalms that quote David asking God, *Why?*— Psalms 10:1; 22:1; 42:9; 44:23–24; 88:14. Try naming your fears and questions. Allow God to comfort you.

TWENTY-FIVE

Freedom

Freedom

Comin' to you live by satellite
From a secret side of town
No mistakin', bonds are shakin'
Walls are breakin' down

You can walk across the border tonight
Unafraid to cross that line
Breathe the fresh air
Kiss the free ground
Leave your dark shadows behind

What will ya do with your new liberation
Open your heart to the God of creation

(Chorus)
Freedom, people cry for freedom
But freedom without Jesus is just another wall

Freedom, give the people freedom
Give the people Jesus

Or they've got nothin' at all
Wise and foolish men alike
Visualizing peace
And it's comin' to pass
Freedom at last . . . it's coming into reach

So don't be fooled by a fools' reward
Hold out for higher ground
'Cause when the time comes
Battles are won
Nothin' gonna hold me down

So don't ya mourn and say how you'll miss me
When you hear the horn, come and go with me

(Repeat Chorus)

FREEDOM by Wayne Watson
© 1990 Word Music (A Div. of WORD MUSIC) and Material Music (Admin. by WORD MUSIC).
All Rights Reserved. Used By Permission.

Freedom without Jesus
is just another wall.

I run in the path of your commands,
for you have set my heart free.
Psalm 119:32

꒛

H

ow many millions of prayers were mercifully answered on that day in 1989 when the great Berlin Wall crumbled and fell? As citizens of free America, living near the end of the twentieth century, we are incapable of fully appreciating how sweet that freedom must have tasted to those who had been denied it so long. I remember the pictures transmitted by satellite. There were celebrations, cheering, and dancing in the streets.

But when the party subsided, the repercussions of freedom began to set in. Unaccustomed to freedom, these newly released "prisoners" were also unaccustomed to the responsibilities of freedom. Sadly, many soon became deeply immersed in human delights that quickly turned into human vice. Many were speedily overcome by their most base desires.

Truly, freedom without Jesus is just another wall.

I can't speak for everyone, but I suppose that the desire for freedom is deeply ingrained in the nature of us all. But the definition of freedom varies greatly from one person to the next. Freedom to a man who works fourteen hours a day under the authority of a relentless boss might be having a few hours during the weekend without anyone telling him what to do. To a mother of five children, freedom may be as simple as a few minutes of peace and quiet or a nice meal at a restaurant with others serving *her*. All of us must be careful, though, that our simple adventures into "well-deserved" freedom don't lead us from the path God has called us to walk.

The cry for freedom in our country comes packaged with many other agendas in tow. One group may claim that freedom is controlling school prayer or denying it altogether. In doing so, they say, they're protecting the freedoms of all by denying the freedoms of a few. The group being silenced (can you really silence prayer?) protests that their freedoms are being threatened. The gang member may feel his or her freedoms are denied through restrictions against certain fashions or specific colors. Rebellious types might enjoy the spotlight as they insist that they have the freedom to publicly burn the American flag, while those who paid a great price for freedom would feel that such a display was a mockery of freedom. Even as you read this, you may be thinking of a few freedom "hot buttons" that make your blood boil.

While many define freedom through a cultural or traditional orientation, true freedom never comes through political or religious institutions. True freedom comes only through relationship with our God and creator. And true freedom involves responsibility.

When the seventeen-year-old son begins to clamor for freedom, he learns that with freedom comes responsibility. If he has the freedom to drive the car, he may have to be responsible for some of the costs of operation and upkeep. If he has the freedom of a later curfew, he is responsible to make wise choices about where he spends his time and the friends he spends it with. So it is with spiritual freedom.

One of the responsibilities of spiritual freedom is *obedience,* and one of the blessings of obedience is knowing that we are on the right track and that we are pleasing God. That knowledge gives us the peace of mind to freely dream big dreams and use all our physical and mental resources to honor him. The psalmist said it beautifully: "I run in the path of your commands, for you have set my heart free" (Ps. 119:32). A train runs swiftly and with ease as long as it stays within the "confines" of the track; we, too, can run with freedom and abandon, as long as we stay in the paths of his commands. A life of obedience is lived joyfully in the presence of the Father, unintimidated by a narrow-thinking world. True freedom is living to please God.

Our freedom comes at great price. The freedoms we enjoy as disciples of Christ cost our Savior's life. God has set our spirits free to live responsibly, obediently, and with compassion as we hold out the freedom of Christ to a world in bondage.

CHAPTER TWENTY-FIVE

PERSONAL REFLECTIONS

1. When you think of freedom, what comes to mind?

2. Have you ever seen freedom abused? How?

3. What responsibilities come with Christian freedom?

4. How can freedom be like staying on the confines of a path?

5. How is "freedom without Jesus just another wall"?

life response

Are there any biblical teachings that seem restrictive to you? Meditate on how those teachings might actually bring you increased freedom if you adhere to them.